ERNEST DOWSON
COLLECTED POEMS

Ernest Dowson
Collected Poems

Edited by

R. K. R. Thornton
with
Caroline Dowson

Birmingham University Press
2003

First published in the United Kingdom by
The University of Birmingham Press,
University of Birmingham,
Edgbaston,
Birmingham, B15 2TT, UK.

ISBN 1-902459-47-4

British Library Cataloguing in Publication data

A CIP catalogue record for this book is available from the British Library

CONTENTS

POÉSIE SCHUBLADE

EARLY AND UNCOLLECTED POEMS

VERSES (1896)

vii

TO ERNEST DOWSON

Of the ways of writing a poem, one way is
Where the sound's what you fashion the sense with; another
Where you try for a mood, not seeking out harmonies.
And they don't come together so often, these ways,
Except as how sometimes the sea's crash is music,
Or the motion expressed in some music's a mood.

That's where Dowson comes in. That's his mood;
And critics go carping along: 'No variety;
He only says one thing: he's in love and wants peace,
But she won't; so he yearns, grows sad, world weary.'
But they see the words circling and ignore their hearing.
Listen! Oh, but there's music in Dowson.

Say what you will, there's more than just Cynara
Stuck like a cherry on top of the nineties,
More than just dabbling in Verlaine and Pater,
And becoming a Catholic as most of the rest did.
It's more than being love-sick for juvenile virgins
And fashionably dying of tuberculosis.

'There are more than two ways,' did I hear? I expected
I'd get that. 'You might be engrossed in the meaning.'
That's just what you would say, too, looking in Dowson
For different themes, when his aim was the losing
Of sense in the calm variation of music.
He only knew one way. But one way sufficed him.

K.T.

INTRODUCTION

In March 1914, the almost-forgotten Nineties poet Theodore Wratislaw, thinking that he might be introduced to Olive Custance, went to the British Museum to prepare by reading her poems. On some whim, he also applied for Ernest Dowson's poems. He recorded his stunned response in a letter to a friend:

> Well, I waded rather drearily through Lady Douglas, and then picked up Dowson, and had a shock. Do you know I now think that Dowson was the finest poet of the time, and that some of his poems rank in the very first line of English poetry? I had known some of his stuff when he was alive — but not much, and I could not read then — nor could I yesterday — the 'Pierrot of the Minute'. I saw him fairly often — a slight, frail, illusive, boy, and I had not appreciated him as I ought to have done. So it came to me as a shock to find how intensely good are some of his poems.
>
> I had to put the book down once or twice — to think what a fool I had been in not seeing his value before: and at last I had to shut it and come away. It may be that my mood now is more attuned to his, or that his tragic life and death have put the stamp of sincerity on what perhaps seemed to be insincere. When I saw him, he always seemed to be light-hearted, a casual, frivolous, yet charming, boy whose chief ambition was to make one go to a cabman's shelter for coffee — which I never did — or to a night-club, which I did once or twice in his society. I offended him once, quite unintentionally and after that he drifted to Brittany and I to penal servitude in Somerset House and I saw him no more.
>
> Some day, some one will discover that Dowson was one of the finest English poets.[1]

That last comment, enriched by the fact that it was from one who had known Dowson, is not uncommon in those who discover his poetry; and it is because of a conviction that a new generation and a new century will wish to read him that this edition has been put together. It will be the business of the introduction to flesh out some of Wratislaw's perceptions.

Ernest Christopher Dowson was born at Lee in Kent on 2 August 1867 and died at Catford on 23 February 1900.

His young parents — his father was 24 and his mother only 18 when he was born — inherited enough income from the dry dock they owned at Limehouse to have a refined way of life, but they also inherited a susceptibility to consumption and so had to pursue health into a variety of European resorts. At Mentone in 1873, they met Robert Louis Stevenson, who took a shine to young Ernest, but found his mother 'not very come-at-able'.[2] Ernest's education was erratic, with a variety of tutors in different languages from time to time replacing his cultured father, who himself nurtured literary ambitions. But, however erratic his education, his familiarity with the ancient and modern languages enabled him to get a place at Oxford, where he read classics at Queen's from October 1886. After five terms, he decided that university life and examinations were not for him and he left, first to try his hand at studying for the Bar — which he also soon abandoned — and then to help in the running of the family business (which may have been in fact the reason he went down).

The dry dock, which in is heyday had brought in a handsome sum, was now suffering from lack of investment and the changing needs of shipping in the Thames. Father and son, unskilled in the art of dock management, nonetheless had to buckle down to the job of bookkeeping and trying to keep the firm afloat. Ernest, however, had other ideas, and having published his first poem and his first story when he was still a student at Oxford, wished to make his way as a writer, and took up an unpaid evening job as sub-editor of a failing literary review called *The Critic*. Its reviewing and its free tickets for plays and music-halls gave Dowson entry to the busy theatrical and literary life of London, but it did not live long into the nineties.

In 1889 he met the Polish restaurant-keeper's daughter who became the lodestar of his life. He had, even as a teenager, always expressed an idealising affection for young girls, collecting pictures of Minnie Terry the child actress for example, but in Adelaide Foltinowicz (whom he and his friends referred to as 'Missie') he finally embodied the ideal irrevocably. He went night after night to the restaurant in Sherwood Street — which his friends did not always find a wonderful eating place either for the food or the ambience — and delighted himself with her company. Back in 1888 he had lamented to his friend Sayle: 'the world is a bankrupt concern and life a play that ought to have been damned the first night. There are, as you say, still books, dogs and little girls of seven years old in it but unhappily, one begins to yawn over the books and the dogs die and, oh Sayle, Sayle, the little girls grow up, and become those very objectionable animals, women'.[3] Now he found himself committed, come what may, to a girl who was eleven when he first met her and just approaching fifteen when he proposed in April 1893. His suit was impossible and she quite understandably refused, but his commitment to her did not waver, as the dedications of his books, the draft title page of his Paris notebook and the dedication page of his copy of his *Dilemmas* testify. This last shows that his consciousness of her importance was restated and revived wherever he went, from its publication to 1899.

By the early 1890s Dowson was beginning to be known among the advanced coterie of writers who gathered round the Century Guild, the Bodley Head and the Rhymers' Club. His stories were published in the *Hobby Horse*, as later they were to be in the *Yellow Book* and the *Savoy*; and his poems were in demand. Dowson contributed the maximum allowance of six poems to each of the Rhymers' Club books and his contributions are among those which make the collections significant.

The Rhymers' Club began to break up after the publication of its second volume, and Dowson's life also began its long relentless disintegration. Adelaide's father died within a week of his proposal to Adelaide. Both his own parents died within six months of each other in late 1894 and early 1895, certainly one but perhaps both suicides. The dock was obviously on its last legs and Dowson moved out, unable to realise any money from its sale. He began his wanderings between London, Paris and Brittany, which left him rootless and not far from penniless for the rest of his life.

In publishing terms, his career perhaps looked more healthy. His novel, *A Comedy of Masks*, written in collaboration with Arthur Moore, was published in 1893. His translation of Zola's *La Terre* was published in 1894. His translation with Teixeira de Mattos of Couperus's *Majesty* was published in 1894. His short stories were collected in *Dilemmas: Studies in Sentiment* in 1895 and his poems in *Verses* in 1896. He continued, despite seriously declining health and the lack of any secure base, to translate for Leonard Smithers, producing *Les liaisons dangeureuses* (1898) and *Memoirs of Cardinal Dubois* (1899) along with the verse translation of Voltaire's eight and a half thousand line scurrilous epic *La Pucelle* (1899) and his second novel written in collaboration with Moore, *Adrian Rome* (1899). But his final collection, *Decorations: in Verse and Prose* (1899), is probably less impressive than his first, being a second gathering from the earlier store which had been picked over for *Verses,* with the addition of a few memorable new poems and five prose poems somewhat in Olive Schreiner's mode.

Adelaide married the German waiter (perhaps he was also a tailor, as her father had been) in 1897 but Dowson remained, as he expressed it in *'Non sum qualis eram . . .'*, true to her in his fashion. A friend, R. H. Sherard, found him early in 1900 looking ill and unkempt and took him home to Catford where he looked after him until he died a few weeks later, aged 32.

That is the bones of his story, but 'The Dowson Legend' makes a more lurid tale. Its four elements are Dowson's womanising; the obverse of that, his idealising of 'Missie'; his abuse of drink and drugs; and his general squalor and disreputableness. A more modern development is to turn scorn of his apparently unreciprocated adoration of a fairly unremarkable girl into an accusation of paedophilia. These topics are part of the sensational and romanticised accounts which attempt to create of Dowson an archetypal *'poète maudit'*. And they are disputed by a group of defenders, who come to his aid in depicting him as a likeable, hard-working, idealistic young man, with some minor flaws and not blessed with good health, who remained faithful to an ideal of innocence.

The first element — Dowson's womanising, with tarts, whores or loose women from the theatres and music-halls — is exemplified in Ezra Pound's line from 'Hugh Selwyn Mauberley': 'Dowson found harlots cheaper than hotels'.[4] Here Pound repeats a tale he probably heard from Yeats or Symons (it is unlikely that he heard it from Victor Plarr, the 'Monsieur Verog' of that part of the poem, since Plarr was one of Dowson's early defenders). Arthur Symons in his 'A Literary Causerie: on a book of Verses' in number 4 of the *Savoy,* and later in the introduction to *Poems* (1905) which is based on the same material, set the tone of these stories: 'As long as he was conscious of himself, there was but one woman for him in the world, and for her he had an infinite tenderness and an infinite respect. When that face faded from him, he saw all the other faces, and he saw no more difference than between sheep and sheep'.[5] Yeats, in his *Autobiographies,* picked up Symons's version and related that 'Sober, he looked on no woman; drunk, he picked the cheapest whore'.[6] The connection with the second element, the idealised form of 'Missie', is already clear. Since the subject of Dowson's most famous poem, '*Non sum qualis eram . . .*' is the rueful recognition that the 'bought red mouth' of the woman with whom he has spent the night does not obliterate the memory of Cynara, it was perhaps inevitable that this account gained currency.

The drug abuse is easier to deal with quickly. Dowson had indeed tried haschisch at Oxford, but it was a brief experiment and not repeated except once or twice in Symons's company. But he did drink and often to excess; that is, when he could afford it, which was certainly not always the case in his later years in France. A letter to Edgar Jepson of 30 July 1894 tells of a celebration after seeing off to her family a sick young woman who had taken an overdose of abortifacient. Dowson consumed seven absinthes that evening, but the letter ends with the comment that 'This morning Goodhart and I were twitching visibly. I feel rather indisposed; and in fact we decided that our grief is sufficiently drowned, and we must spend a few days on nothing stronger than lemonade and strychnine'.[7] In other words, Dowson was a habitual convivial drinker, who overdid it often, so that it begins to seem pathological. By the time he was working in France in the late 1890s he would be too poor to indulge much. 'I certainly have no intention of drinking any monies,' he wrote to Leonard Smithers. 'Food has lately been too scarce, even tobacco'.[8] There is nonetheless an element of the desire to suffer in his drinking and in his self-neglect.

As far as his disreputableness goes, and the 'love of the sordid' which Symons describes, it is evident that Dowson was capable of washing and dressing smartly enough to satisfy at times the dandy Teixeira de Mattos; but he became increasingly neglectful of his appearance and certainly did not look after his clothes, his teeth or himself. Those who met him in France and on his visits back to England in the later 1890s usually comment on his unkempt appearance.

A number of friends and supporters have objected to the too-sensational picture of Dowson, and their accounts are needed to balance our view. Edgar Jepson in 1907 attempted to correct Symons's picture in 'The Real Ernest Dowson', in the *Academy* and again in his *Memories of a Victorian* (1933). Victor Plarr published an account of Dowson which he hoped would give a kinder picture of his friend in *Ernest Dowson, 1888-1897: Reminiscences, Unpublished Letters and Marginalia* (1914). There he claimed that there were 'two Dowsons — one the vexed and torn spirit of the biographers, of Mr Sherard and Mr Arthur Symons, the other a Dowson *intime*, known, I venture to think, to very few, but by those few greatly loved' (p.9). An Oxford friend, W.R. Thomas, gave an account of 'Ernest Dowson at Oxford' in the *Nineteenth Century* of April 1928. And most clearly Desmond Flower in his edition of the *Poetical Works* in 1934 (and 1950 and 1967) and in the *Letters of Ernest Dowson* (1967), which he edited with Henry Maas, has put the evidence before us on which we can make a judgement of the different aspects of Dowson's character.[9]

Dowson's love for a young girl has of course its potentially sinister side, which has to be faced. We do not wish to fall into a crude summary such as that offered by Bernard Richards in the *Missing Persons* addition to the *Dictionary of National Biography* (1993):

> Through the letters and poetry there runs a strong current of paedophilia, which has an erotic strain, but it is tempered by a humane appreciation of the freshness and generosity of children not yet tainted by the manners of society.

This seems to have a blunt idea of both Dowson and paedophilia.[10] The problem is of course, what we mean by 'paedophilia', and we need to distinguish between someone who has a sexual interest in children and a passionate admirer of innocence. If having a special regard for the innocence of childhood amounts to paedophilia, then many of us, not least Christ, are tainted. But Dowson himself was anxious that his love for Adelaide should not be misconstrued and threatened, and he was particularly concerned when he read of a scandal in August 1891 when Adelaide was thirteen. A journalist called Newton had struck up a relationship with a young girl called Lucy Pearson (ironically in Fountain Court), and their relationship deepened until they ran away together when she was fifteen. They were apprehended and Newton was given a six-month sentence for unlawfully taking her and for being improperly intimate with her (a crime which was new to the statute books). It is worth quoting Dowson's letter extensively:

> I feel just at present, as though everything that was at all charming and pleasant were entirely and irretrievably over. It makes me furious — but I must admit, that I am so unfortunately constituted as to allow small miseries almost to madden me. I have had a moral shock since yesterday, which has racked me ever since with an infinite horror that I may be misunderstood in the only thing that I really care about, by the only people to whom it matters. As ill luck would have it I came across the Star yesterday and read a most disgusting story of a disgusting person, which I suppose is a notorious scandal that one has escaped by being in Brittany.

The worst of it was, that it read like a sort of foul and abominable travesty of — pah, what is the good of hunting for phrases. You must know what I mean, and how I am writhing. I imagine all the comments and analogies which one's kind friends will draw, and unfortunately I can't help feeling that even her people — and mine, as far as that goes — might take alarm and suspect my motives. And yet I swear there never was a man more frantically opposed to the corruption of innocence — even where women are concerned — than I am. Unfortunately the excellence of my conscience doesn't make any difference. This beastly thing has left a sort of slimy trail over my holy places.[11]

It is not that Dowson protests too much here, as Jad Adams suggests, but that he recognises his need as a pathological need for the ideal, and understands that this need is not sexual. There is no clear evidence in the accounts of friends or in his letters of any sexual abuse of children nor any desire for it in his poems.

He was quite capable of adult sexual union, as many of his acquaintances and many of his letters testify, but something drove him to seek a different sort of union, a merging with an innocent loved one, even perhaps in death. A psychoanalyst might hypothesise that some difficulty with his young mother (perhaps the 'un-come-at-able-ness' that Stevenson noted) left him longing for the bliss of the merged relationship of early infancy, which it seems she could not offer. Right from the earliest of his writings which we have, written when he was in his late teens, he had this same longing for fusion with a love object, which finds its expression in his early poems, and is finally focussed on Adelaide. Whether he planned to marry her or not (and his proposal when she was just about to turn fifteen and her father was near death seems designed to fail), I agree with Arthur Symons, who wrote that 'there was a sort of virginal devotion, as to a Madonna; and I think, had things gone happily, to a conventionally happy ending, he would have felt (dare I say?) that his ideal had been spoilt'.[12] Part of himself, that part which wrote his last prose poem, knew she could not fulfil what he deluded himself she promised; but part of himself could not give up on the wish that she could. Whilst the paedophile looks to the child for sexual gratification, Dowson looks for eternal love. It is the expression of that distinction which helps to give Dowson's poems their desperate charm.

Dowson did see the draft of Symons's article for the *Savoy* and made few objections, merely saying that Symons was right in assuming his 'complete indifference as to what things may be said of me'. He did wish him to tone down the phrases which suggested the 'too hopelessly disreputable', but was charmed with the way Symons dealt with his love of Adelaide and admitted that he had 'always had, alas! too much of that "swift, disastrous and suicidal energy" which destroyed our dear and incomparable Verlaine'.[13]

If Dowson was his own worst enemy in preserving his reputation, he was also his own worst enemy when it came to blowing the trumpet for his verses. He kept them in a drawer and offered them to friends and from time to time to magazines, which sometimes took them and sometimes sent them back with a polite refusal. But he was much more concerned to make his mark as a writer of prose, which he preferred to his verse. There are so many witnesses to this opinion that one can scarcely doubt that he seriously believed it. He said to Frank Harris while speaking of Poe that 'He was a master of both prose and verse . . . his prose better than his verse, as mine is'.[14] A contemporary of his at Oxford, W. R. Thomas,[15] reported that Dowson wished to be a writer of prose rather than poetry and said that 'poetry, when it came, was an outburst, a digression'. The first editor of his poems, Arthur Symons, wrote that 'Dowson was the only poet I ever knew who cared more for his prose than his verse'.[16]

What Dowson writes in his private letters bears out the little regard he had for his poems. It is a repeated refrain. 'I don't pretend to write verse seriously', he wrote in January 1889 to his close friend and collaborator Arthur Moore.[17] He voiced the same opinion when he wrote to Charles Sayle on 1 April 1889 that 'I have a sonnet in this month's "Temple Bar": that is all and that is nothing for I have never done any more than play with verse'.[18] To Sayle again, in response to a poem addressed to him in November 1889 he writes: 'I have begun to accept my limitations and will not pay you the sorry compliment of returning *verses* for your *poem*'.[19] Writing probably of the 'Villanelle of Acheron' and again apropos of Poe, he says to Arthur Moore: 'My latest Valueless Villanelle I enclose you. It has been sent to "Atalanta" and I await its return with a philosophic resignation which I would I could muster equally where my prose is in question'.[20] Again to Moore on 20 March 1891 he says he has been 'writing verses, in the manner of the French "symbolists": verses making for mere sound, and music, with just a suggestion of sense, or hardly that; a vague Verlainesque emotion. They are not successful enough to send you'.[21] He wrote to John Gray, in reference to 'Impenitentia Ultima' that: 'I have a short story in the forthcoming new "Savoy" which I should like you to read, also a poem, but that is rather pommade'.[22] And to Plarr he wrote in August 1893: 'I do not even attempt to write any longer, not even verses'.[23] Ironically, although he was known and wished to be known at university as a writer of prose, it was a poem which was his first published work: 'Sonnet to a little Girl' in *London Society* for November 1886.

One can offer some suggestions as to why it was that he expressed a lower opinion for his verse than for his prose. Partly it was because poetry came so easily to him; it was the natural expression of his deepest feelings and came without the effort and concentration of his prose. Partly he wished to protect from too much scrutiny the intimate self which is expressed there. Partly, of course, it was his sincere commitment to writing something new and serious in prose, and perhaps his father's unsuccessful attempts to publish prose also had some effect on his valuation of his work. Whatever the reason behind his low valuation of his poetry, as Arthur Symons says, 'he was wrong, and it is not by his prose that he will live'.[24]

Although his composition of verse was fairly easy and natural, it is not that he simply accepted the first thing that came into his head. The revisions and deletions in his notebook indicate clearly that he knew how to revise and improve his work, and the reader can follow the substantive changes in the notes we provide. Indeed there is hardly a change which he makes which is not for the better. His ear was impeccable.

Value it or not, he did preserve his poetry carefully. We still have a notebook in which he transcribed his poems, and we even have the title page for one of the notebooks which he subsequently used, which reads: 'Fragments by Ernest Dowson / Copied out. Paris — to be worked up' (see pages 1-6). The best, and indeed apart from his letters almost the only record of Dowson's growing talent as a poet is this small notebook which he used until it was full in December 1891. Into this he transcribed 21 pages of poems in 1886 or early 1887 and thenceforward made copies of his poems as he wrote them. It is a neat, leather-bound volume with marbled endpapers and it cost half a crown, which was quite expensive for a blank book. He obviously intended it to be a serious repository for his poems and he kept it neatly and carefully. He wrote almost exclusively on the rectos of the volume, using the versos only for occasional annotation and experimentation, often adding information about the publication or sometimes rejection of his work either beneath the poem or on the verso opposite. Some of the pages are torn out, but whether to give to a friend or to send to a publisher to save the time of copying out it is impossible to say. What was on some of the torn-out pages can be established by checking with notes on remaining pages, but in the case of the first pages which have been torn out, the remaining clues do not point to any extant poem.

Dowson referred to this book in a letter to Victor Plarr of 5 March 1891.[25] They are planning a small book of their poems, ten by each author, to be ready for when they have some money to finance the printing. Dowson discusses proposed titles, liking 'Vineleaf and Violet' and 'Rose and Pine', and says that 'I have been looking over my "Poesie Schublade" as represented by a small MSS book and it will be with difficulty that I shall find ten worthy of the company of the best of yours'.

'Poésie Schublade' or 'Drawer poetry', especially in that protective covering of two languages, suggests something of the way in which Dowson viewed his poems. But the neatness and persistence of the notebook rather contradict his deprecatory comments. It is true that Dowson worked hard at his prose and that his declared models were usually writers of prose, but verse came naturally, and it was valued by his friends, if not always by the critics and publishers. Even if it was only to keep in a drawer, his poetry was carefully kept.

'Poésie Schublade', then, records and defines Dowson's development as a poet from 1886 to the end of 1891, and it seemed worth presenting Dowson as a growing poet rather than to relegate the material of his apprentice years to an appendix. The difficulty is that many of the poems from the notebook were used in *Verses* and in *Decorations*, so that there would be a danger of substantial duplication. The process we have decided on is to begin with a description of the Flower notebook, and to indicate which poems from it were published in his lifetime and which were not. We present first the poems which Dowson chose not to publish — whether he thought they were too poor or too private it is impossible to say — and then print in order of publication his three published volumes and his verse translation: *Verses* (1896), his 'Dramatic Phantasy' *The Pierrot of the Minute,* written and performed in 1892 and published in 1897, the two cantos of Voltaire's *La Pucelle* which were solely his, and *Decorations* (1899), with the small number of poems which lie outside these five groups included after his early work.

The sequence of poems which we have chosen is thus not strictly chronological. We are presenting the contents of *Verses* and *Decorations* in the order in which they were first printed, since Dowson evidently had some design in mind. *Verses*, for example, opens with 'They are not long' as an epigraph before the 'Preface: for Adelaide'; he follows this with the dedicatory 'A Coronal *With His songs and Her days to His Lady and to Love*' before the reiteration of the volume title *Verses* which introduces 'Nuns of the Perpetual Adoration'. The book ends with a note of hope in 'Chanson Sans Paroles'. *Decorations* begins with an epigraphic poem about 'Love's Aftermath', which at one point was to be the title of the volume; the collection ends its verse section with the valedictory 'A Last Word' and ends its prose section with the realization that 'Some say, moreover, that her tower is not of ivory and that she is not even virtuous nor a princess.' The relationship with Adelaide is central to Dowson, and his shaping of the books to comment on it seems deliberate. It would be wrong to disarrange this obvious design.

The influences on Dowson's poetry were many and various, but some are very obvious. Swinburne provided strong hints in metrics and in certain patterns of phrase such as antithetical pairs (Swinburne's 'lilies and languors of virtue' and Dowson's 'days of wine and roses' or 'the weeping and the laughter'). Tennyson showed an exactness of word which the French might strive for. Pater provided a mood and sometimes a Latin word or phrase which attracted Dowson's fancy (*umbratilis*, or *domnulam meam*). Baudelaire gave encouragement to look at the subterranean impulses of human nature in his art. Verlaine showed how to write exquisite lyrics with grace, delicacy and music in his wistful measure. And classical authors, particularly Virgil, Propertius, Horace and Catullus, gave him a model in the placing of words.

Perhaps the most important gift of these influences lies in their very variety. The gusto of Swinburne's metrics was moderated by the different French rhythms of Baudelaire and Verlaine and the quantity-based verse of the Latin masters. The sum total was a new sound in English verse. W. B. Yeats recognised this when he wrote that 'For long I only knew Dowson's *O Mors*, to quote but the first words of its long title, and his *Villanelle of Sunset* from his reading, and it was because of the desire to hold them in my hand that I suggested the first *Book of the Rhymers' Club*. They were not speech but perfect song, though song for the speaking voice'.[26] T. S. Eliot also perceived this novelty in Dowson and wrote, in response to a suggestion that he might have found the phrase 'Falls the shadow' in Dowson's 'Cynara', that 'The derivation had not occurred to my mind, but I believe it to be correct, because the lines ... have always run in my head, and because I regard Dowson as a poet whose technical innovations have been underestimated'.[27] Eliot indicated that this is not a passing opinion since, when he contributed a preface for Maurice Lindsay's *John Davidson: a selection of his Poems* (1961), he wrote of Davidson's 'Thirty Bob a Week' that it 'seems to me the only poem in which Davidson freed himself completely from the poetic diction of English verse of his time (just as *Non Sum Qualis Eram* seems to me the one poem in which, by a slight shift of rhythm, Ernest Dowson freed himself).[28]

To see a brief glimpse of the way Dowson's memory worked in making poems, take a passage from Swinburne's 'A Leave-Taking':

> Let us go hence, my songs; she will not hear.
> Let us go hence together without fear;
> Keep silence now, for singing-time is over,
> And over all old things and all things dear.
> She loves not you nor me as all we love her.
> Yea, though we sang as angels in her ear,
> She would not hear.[29]

This is obviously rich ground for Dowson to mine for his poems. The first phrase comes in the last sonnet 'Of a little girl' (p.25 and again p.207). An adaptation comes in 'Ere I go hence' (p.38), which also uses the stanza form of Swinburne's poem. But when Dowson converts his echoes into a sonnet, and works on them (see the notes to 'A Last Word'), the result is a poem whose desolate power is both invigorating and despairing. It is his own music.

We hope that a new generation of readers will be able to enjoy Dowson's poetry and be able to say, as Wilde wrote to Dowson:

> Tonight I am going to read your poems — your lovely lyrics
> — words with wings you write always.[30]

Notes

1. *The Search for Wratislaw*, ed. R. K. R. Thornton (Eighteen Nineties Society, 2003), p.34.
2. Quoted by Jad Adams in *Madder Music, Stronger Wine*, from the *Letters of Robert Louis Stevenson*, vol. I 1854-74 (New Haven, 1994), 22-29 November 1873.

3.   *New Letters from Ernest Dowson*, ed Desmond Flower (Whittington Press, 1984), p.5.
4.   In the 'Siena mi fe; disfecemi Maremma' section of 'Hugh Selwyn Mauberley (Life and Contacts)', Ezra Pound, *Personae* (Faber, 1952), p.202.
5.   *The Poems of Ernest Dowson*, ed. Arthur Symons (John Lane, 1905), p.xv.
6.   W. B. Yeats, *Autobiographies* (Macmillan, 1980), p.399, but repeating almost verbatim the account of p.312.
7.   *The Letters of Ernest Dowson,* ed. Desmond Flower and Henry Maas (Cassell, 1967), p.307.
8.   *Letters*, p.415.
9.   This is only a brief summary. There were other apologists, important among whom were John Gawsworth in *The Dowson Legend* in 1939 and Mark Longaker in his biographies of 1943, 1945 and 1967.
10.   This entry in the *DNB* also says that '"Youth" is an important poem on the loss of childhood'. Dowson did not write a poem called 'Youth' and one must assume that 'Growth' is meant.
11.   *Letters*, p.213.
12.   *The Poems of Ernest Dowson*, introduction, p.xiv.
13.   *Letters*, pp.371-2. The whole letter is vital to an understanding of Dowson's attitudes.
14.   Quoted in *The Stories of Ernest Dowson*, ed. Mark Longaker (W. H. Allen, 1947), p.1.
15.   'Ernest Dowson at Oxford', *The Nineteenth Century*, April 1928.
16.   *The Poems of Ernest Dowson*, introduction, p.xxii.
17.   *Letters*, p.26.
18.   ibid, p.58.
19.   *New Letters*, p.13.
20.   1 June 1890, *Letters*, p.150.
21.   *Letters*, p.190.
22.   December 1895, *Letters* p. 324.
23.   *Letters*, p.286.
24.   *The Poems of Ernest Dowson*, introduction, p.xxii.
25.   *Letters*, p.187.
26.   *Autobiographies*, p.301.
27.   *TLS*, 10 January 1935.
28.   *John Davidson: a selection of his Poems, ed.* Maurice Lindsay (Hutchinson, 1961), p.[xi].
29.   *The Poems of Algernon Charles Swinburne* (Chatto and Windus, 1912), vol. I, p.52. A more extensive discussion of Dowson's poems can be found in R. K. R. Thornton, *The Decadent Dilemma*, pp.71-107, and in the books and articles listed in G. A . Cevasco's bibliography.
30.   *The Complete Letters of Oscar Wilde*, ed. Merlin Holland and Rupert Hart-Davis (Fourth Estate, 2000), p.908.

CHRONOLOGY

1867, August 2:	Born at Lee in Kent.
1867-	Family journeys in search of health in France, Italy and Switzerland.
1873, November:	Meets Robert Louis Stevenson in Hôtel du Pavillon in Mentone.
1870s/early 1880s:	Irregular though in patches deep education.
1878, 13 April:	Ellen Adelaide Mary Foltinowicz born.
1886, October to March 1888:	Attends Oxford University, Queen's College. Moves out of college after first year to 5 Grove Street.
1886:	Begins to enter his poems in his 'Poésie Schublade'.
1886, November:	First poem published in *London Society*
1887:	Begins collaboration on novels with Arthur Moore.
1888, January:	His first story 'Souvenirs of an Egoist' published in *Temple Bar*.
1888, early:	Meets Victor Plarr.
1888:	Begins to read for the Bar but the process abandoned by October.
1888 onwards:	Helps father in dock.
1889, from April:	Works for *The Critic*.
1889:	Experiments with Lena, then with Bertha van Raalte
1889, 1 November:	Meets Adelaide Foltinowicz in 'Poland'.
1890:	First visit to Brittany, which, if anywhere, he regarded as home.
1890 onwards:	Publishes in the *Hobby Horse*.
1891, 6 February:	Writes *'Non sum qualis eram . . .'*
1891-4:	Active in the Rhymers' Club, with Lionel Johnson, Yeats, Arthur Symons, etc. Contributes maximum of six poems to each of two Rhymers' Club collections, in 1892 and 1894.
1891, 25 Sept:	Is received into the Roman Catholic Church.
1892, October:	*Pierrot of the Minute* commissioned by W. T. Peters; performed on 22 November at Chelsea Town Hall.
1893:	Publication of *A Comedy of Masks*
1893:	Applies for librarianship post at Newington.
1893, April:	Proposes to Adelaide but is refused.

1893, 24 April:	Death of Joseph Foltinowicz, Adelaide's father.
1893, November:	Visit of Verlaine to London.
1894:	Publication of translation of Zola's *La Terre*.
1894:	Publishes in the *Yellow Book*.
1894:	Completes translation of Couperus's *Majesty* with Teixeira de Mattos.
1894, 15 August:	Death of his father, Alfred Dowson, perhaps suicide.
1895, 4 February:	Suicide of Annie Dowson, his mother.
1895:	Publication of *Dilemmas: Studies in Sentiment*.
1895:	Meets Leonard Smithers, who would publish much of his subsequent work.
1895:	Begins his peregrinations around Europe: Brussels; Paris.
1895-6:	Collaborates with Greene and Hillier in translation of Muther's *History of Modern Painting*.
1896:	At Pont-Aven. Back in England in November.
1896:	Publishes in the *Savoy*.
1896:	Translation of Balzac's *La Fille aux yeux d'or*.
1896:	*Verses* published.
1897:	*The Pierrot of the Minute* published
1897:	Moves into rooms at 19 Sherwood Street, where Adelaide lived.
1897, April:	With Charles Conder to Arques-la-Bataille and resumes friendship with Oscar Wilde when he is released from Reading Gaol. Returns to England in August. Holiday in Ireland and then back to Paris.
1897, 26 Sept:	Adelaide marries Augustus Noelte at the Bavarian Church.
1898:	Back to London, then holiday in Limerick. Translation of Choderlos de Laclos' *Les liaisons dangeureuses*.
1899:	Back in Paris. Translation of Voltaire's *La Pucelle,*. Returns to London in late summer.
1899:	Translation of *Memoirs of Cardinal Dubois* by Paul Lacroix
1899:	*Decorations* published.
1899:	*Adrian Rome* published.
1900, 23 February:	Dies in R. H. Sherard's house at Catford, aged 32.

A NOTE ON THE TEXT.

We follow the text of the first edition of each of the four major books, since they were what Dowson would have had the chance to see in proof, and over which he would have been careful. Even as late as June 1899, Dowson could write to Smithers that 'the poems what with arranging and *redigeant* have taken up all my time' (*Letters*, p.414). We have checked all poems against the accessible manuscripts.

In the case of the notebook poems, we have gone back to the notebook in the Pierpont Morgan Library in New York and scrupulously checked all the information it provides. We have tried to follow Dowson's pattern of indentation, but it sometimes seems erratic or unclear. At times it begins by following the pattern of the rhyme but grows less distinct as the poem continues. We have tended to follow the pattern of the rhymes, which is his more frequent practice.

Notes of variants, particularly of punctuation, are selective. Since many of the texts of poems sent to friends are available in the *Letters* and elsewhere, and because we are not persuaded that Dowson set great store by punctuation, we have not noted such changes, but we have indicated where the variant versions can be found. We have usually expanded his ampersands.

We hope we have annotated Dowson in a reader-friendly manner, noting substantial changes, bringing the notes up to date and extending the range of his work available. In the case of one poem, we offer two versions, the first and the last, to indicate the nature of Dowson's revisions (see pp.25 and 207).

After three years of amassing a large amount of small detail, we are all too conscious that some errors may have crept in, and we would be delighted to be informed of any corrections which could improve any future edition.

ACKNOWLEDGEMENTS

We would like to pay tribute to earlier Dowson scholars, and especially to the late Desmond Flower, whose editions of the *Poetical Works* and the *Letters* are indispensable resources for anyone working on Dowson. We would like to thank the Pierpont Morgan Library, New York, for permission to use manuscript MA 1480, the Flower Notebook; and all the libraries and librarians who have contributed in their efficient, quiet and necessary way, particularly those at the Pierpont Morgan Library in New York, the Berg Collection in the New York Public Library, the British Library, the Bodleian, the Robinson Library of the University of Newcastle upon Tyne, and the Library of the Newcastle upon Tyne Literary and Philosophical Society. Many others have helped and we would like to thank: Hilary Gates, Tom Cain, Daniel De Simone, Roger Dobson, Nick Granger-Taylor, Steven Halliwell, Mark Samuels Lasner, Christine Nelson, Dr. Jakob Wisse and our publisher Alec McAulay, who has been tolerant of delay and generous with help.

POÉSIE SCHUBLADE
A SUMMARY OF THE FLOWER NOTEBOOK

The Flower notebook is manuscript MA 1480 in the Pierpont Morgan Library, New York. It is a black leather-bound volume measuring 7 by 4.5 inches. It has 77 leaves with extra pages from other notebooks loosely inserted. The pagination is Dowson's and he has numbered the rectos only. Although the first two pages have been torn out, his numbering begins at 2. The writing is in ink unless stated otherwise. Up to p.21 the hand and the ink are consistent, as if copied out at one time.

Selections were made from this volume both for *Verses* and for *Decorations*. We indicate below with bold type and the letter *V* or *D* which poems were later used in those volumes, sometimes under different titles; they will be printed in the present volume only once, in their sequence in the published collections. Those he chose not to publish will be printed here in their order in the notebook.

Dowson usually left the versos blank, but later used them to annotate the poem on the opposite recto with corrections or details of where it had been sent or published, so we note the contents of the versos below *along with* the content of the opposite recto to which they refer.

Front endpaper: 'To Cynara', in pencil.
1:     Torn out leaving initial letters of lines on the stub. These do not match any known poem of Dowson's.
1A: Torn out.
2:    'A Mosaic', stanzas 1-3.
3:    'A Mosaic' concluded, stanza 4.
     'Hymn to Aphrodite' ['Libera Me', *D*], stanzas 1-4.
4:    **'Hymn to Aphrodite'**, stanzas 5-7.
     'Requiem', stanza 1 and three lines of stanza 2.

1

5: 'Requiem', further 3 lines of stanza 2 and 2 concluding stanzas.

'Potnia Thea', 4 line stanza.

6: 'Potnia Thea', 5 stanzas.

7: 'Potnia Thea', concluding 3 stanzas, dated 'Aug. 1886.'

'Rondeau' ('Could you forget, put out of mind'), lines 1-8.

8: 'Rondeau', concluding 7 lines.

'Rondeau' ('In Autumn when the leaf is sere'), crossed out. A trial line for the rondeau opposite on 7v is deleted.

9: 'Sonnets/ I. / In Memoriam. H. C. ob. Feb. 24. 1886'.

10: 'Sonnets/ II / Novalis'.

11: 'Sonnets/ Of a Little Girl/ (i)'.

12: 'Sonnets/ Of a Little Girl/ (ii)'.

13: 'Sonnets/ Of a Little Girl/ (iii)'.

14: 'Sonnets/ Of a Little Girl/ (iv)', dated '1885'. Annotated in pencil 'published London Society'.

15: 'Sonnets/ Of a Little girl/ (v)'.

'[Sonnets/ Of a Little girl/] (vi)', lines 1-5.

16: '(vi)' continued, lines 6-14.

'[Sonnets/ Of a Little girl/] (vii)', lines 1-9.

17: '(vii)' continued, lines 10-14.

'[Sonnets/ Of a Little girl/] **(viii). Epilogue'** ['A Last Word', *D*]; redraftings of lines 7ff on 16v.

18: 'La jeunesse n'a q'un temps'.

19: 'Song of the XIXth Century'.

'A Lullaby', lines 1-6.

20: 'Lullaby' concluded, lines 7-15.

'Spleen', three stanzas, crossed through.

21: 'Spleen' concluded, stanzas 4-7.

22: 'After Many Years', stanzas 1-3.

23: 'After Many Years' concluded, stanzas 4-7.

24: 'Praeterita', lines 1-20.

25: 'Praeterita' concluded, lines 21-40.

26: Missing.

27: Missing. **['Moritura', *D*]**

28: Top half torn away [**'Moritura'** concluded] leaving 'ndon Society. March 1887'.

'Adios!', lines 1-10.

29: 'Adios!' concluded, lines 11-20.

'A Song for Spring Time' ['In Spring', *D*], lines 1-7.

30: **'A Song for Spring Time'** concluded, lines 8-15. Alternative line suggested on 29v.
'Seraphita-Seraphitūs', lines 1-12.

31: 'Seraphita-Seraphitūs' concluded. Lower piece of page cut out.

32: **'Sonnet / April' ['My Lady April', *V*]**, dated 'April. 1888.', with pencil note: 'published Temple Bar. April. 1889'. Dowson tries out the spelling of 'wantoness' on 31v.

33: 'It is Finished'.

34: 'Ere I go Hence'.

35: 'Transit Gloria', stanzas 1-5.

36: 'Transit Gloria' continued, stanzas 6-10.

37: 'Transit Gloria' concluded, stanzas 11-16, dated 'May. 19. 1887.'

38: 'Sonnet/ To Nature', dated 'Aug. 1887.'

39: 'Awakening', stanzas 1-4.

40: 'Awakening' concluded, stanzas 5-7, dated 'May 1888.'
'Lullaby',lines 1-8.

41: 'Lullaby' concluded, lines 9-24, dated 'May.1888.' On 40v an alternative word for l.10 of 'Lullaby' and the note: 'Rejected – Atalanta'.

42: 'The Old Year', lines 1-20.

43: 'The Old Year' concluded, lines 21-40, dated '31/12/88.'

44: 'The New Year', lines 1-18.

45: 'The New Year' concluded, lines 19-24, dated 'Jan. 1889.'
'From the Icelandic' (title corrected from 'Thalassios'), lines 1-7. Pencil note on 44v: 'Rejected - Temple Bar'

46: 'From the Icelandic' continued, lines 8-21.

47: 'From the Icelandic' concluded, lines 22-35, dated 'April 1889.'

48: Missing.

49: 'Love's Epilogue', lines 1-16.
A pen draft of **'This is the wisdom of the wise' ['Wisdom', *D*]** across 47v and 49 shows that page 48 had been removed before Dowson drafted that poem. There is a pencil note on 47v saying 'Rejected — Blackwood — Belgravia', which almost certainly refers to the removed poem from p.48 since the pencil note on 49v , which can only refer to 'Love's Epilogue' reads 'Rejected — English Illustrated/Chambers Journal'.

50: 'Love's Epilogue' concluded, lines 17-32, dated 'Aug 2. 1889.'

51: **'To Hélène/ A Rondeau' ['Beyond', *D*]**, dated 'Aug. 1889.'

Annotated in pencil 'Temple Bar' and on opposite page 'Published. / Sept. 1893. Temple Bar'.

52: 'Rondeau / Hélène', dated 'Aug. 1889.'

53: **'Rondeau'** ['Jadis', *D*], dated 'Aug. 24th./ 89'. Title suggested in pencil in a later hand.

54: 'Roundel / To Hélène', dated 'Oct. 27th. 89.'

55: **'To His Mistress'** [*D*], lines 1-16. Pencil comment on 54v opposite: '*Rejected — Longmans — / Universal Review'

56: **'To His Mistress'** concluded, lines 17-24, dated 'Dec. 2. 1889.' 'Rondel', dated 'Feb. 4. '90'.

57: Missing. [probably **'The Dead Child'** ll.1-15]. The annotation 'Accepted "Atalanta" / Oct.1890' in pencil on 56v refers to a poem on the missing pages 57 and 58 rather than to the villanelle on p.59 which the note now faces. **'The Dead Child'** [*D*], for which there is no known manuscript, was the only poem Dowson published in *Atalanta*, and is likely to be the poem from pp.57 and 58; its length would fit two of Dowson's pages.

58: Missing [probably **'The Dead Child'** ll. 16-30].

59: **'Villanelle'** ['Villanelle of Acheron', *D*], dated '25/3/90'.

60: Missing. Perhaps another villanelle like **'Villanelle of His Lady's Treasures'** [*V*]? In a letter to Moore of 1 June 1890 he reports that 'My latest Valueless Villanelle I enclose you. It has been sent to 'Atalanta' and I await its return' (*Letters*, p.150).

61: Missing.

62: **'Villanelle'** ['Villanelle of Sunset', *V*], dated 'June 2 / 1890'. The note 'Rejected Atalanta' in pencil on 59v again refers to a poem from the missing pages rather than to this poem, which the note now faces.

63: **'Amor Umbratilis'** [*V*], lines 1-16, the title added later in ink. On 62v opposite are the notes: 'Rejected "English Illustrated"/ Accepted "Century Guild Hobby Horse" / Oct 10th. 1890. / Pub. C. G. H. H. Oct. 1891 / & / Book of Rhymers Club 1892'.

64: **'Amor Umbratilis'** concluded, lines 17-20, dated 'Sept 18th. 1890'. **'A Dedication: with his poems and Her Days to His Lady; and to Love'** ['A Coronal', *V*], lines 1-9. Note opposite on p.63v reads: 'Rejected: Longmans Mag.'

65: **'A Dedication . . .'** concluded, dated 'Oct 16th. 90'.

66: **'Ad** Domnulam Suam' [*V*], lines 1-16.

67: **'Ad Domnulam Suam'** concluded, lines 17-20, dated 'Oct 18th'.

1890'. Two lines in different ink on facing page 66v are deleted:
'In vain we cross the seas, change lands,
In search of that we know not.'

68: **'A little while to walk with thee, dear child'** ['Transition', *D*],
dated 'Dec. 26. 90'. The final correction for the last line is on 67v.

69: 'Discedam, explebo numerum, reddarque tenebris', dated
'Jan 31. '91', title in pencil, with new last line in pencil on 68v.

70: **'Non sum qualis eram bonae sub regno Cynarae'** [*V*], stanzas
1-3, with pencil comment on 69v: 'Hobby Horse — / April 1891
—'

71: **'Non sum qualis eram bonae sub regno Cynarae'** concluded,
stanza 4, dated 'Feb 7ᵗʰ. 1891.' Variant half-line on 70v.

72: **'Ursulines of the Perpetual Adoration'** ['Nuns of the Perpetual
Adoration', *V*], lines 1-16. Two minor alterations and pencil
annotation on 71v opposite: 'Hobby Horse / April 1891.'

73: **'Ursulines of the Perpetual Adoration'** concluded, lines 17-32,
dated 'Feb 10.1891'. On 72v is a redraft of stanza 5 of 'Ursulines',
and in pencil the phrase: 'Procul o procul este profani'.

74: **'Vanitas'** [*V*], dated 'March 19 / 91'. On 73v is the quotation:
'"On my eyelids is the shadow of Death" / Job xvi. 16'.

75: Missing.

76: **'O Mors / quam amara est memoria tua homini Pacem habenti
in substantiis suis'** [*V*], dated '28 / April / 91'.

77: **'Carthusians'** [*D*], lines 1-16; redraft of stanza 4 on 76v.

78: **'Carthusians'** concluded, lines 17-36, dated '27 / May / 91'.

79: **'Claire: la lune!'** ['Flos Lunae', *V*], dated 'July 20ᵗʰ. 1891'.
Annotated in pencil on 78v opposite: 'Century Guild Hobby
Horse'.

80: **'From the French of Paul Verlaine ("Tears fall within my
heart")'** ['After Paul Verlaine, I', *D*], dated 'Sept 8ᵗʰ. 1891.'

81: Missing ['Colloque Sentimental', 'After Paul Verlaine, II', *D*].
On 80v are two female profiles and the line 'So through the
madding oats they wandered', a variant of a line in **'Colloque
Sentimental'**, which poem was presumably on the missing p.81.

82: Missing, perhaps another Verlaine translation.

83: **'You would have understood me had you waited'** [*V*], lines 1-
16, with epigraph added in indelible pencil.

84: **'You would have understood me had you waited'** concluded,
lines 17-28, dated 'Sept 13ᵗʰ. 1891'.

85:   'Against My Lady Burton: on her burning the last writing of her
      dead husband', lines 1-20.
86:   'Against My Lady Burton' concluded, lines 21-26, dated 'Nov.
      10ᵗʰ. 1891'.
      'Vain Resolves' [*V*], lines 1-11.
87:   **'Vain Resolves'** concluded, lines 12-21, dated 'Dec. 3ʳᵈ. 1891'.
87v: In pencil the words: 'To E.A. Jepson / Edgar Jepson'; then in ink:
      'Where the'; then in a different ink 'Ernest Dowson' and the
      sketch of a face followed by some squiggles.
Rear endpaper: **'Marguerites. A Villanelle'** ['Villanelle of
      Marguerites', *V*], dated 'Dec 31ˢᵗ. 91'.

Loose pages:

a.   A title page on same paper as b, c, and d below, unnumbered:
      'Fragments / by Ernest Dowson / Copied out. Paris — to be
      worked up. / Nov. 1897.' and then the verse:
          'Tu mihi sola domus, tu Cynthia, sola parens
              Omnia tu nostrae tempora laetitiae.
          Seu tristis veniam, seu contra laetus amicis
              Quidquid ero, dicam: "Cynthia cause fuit".
                                        Propertius I. 12.'
      Actually Propertius I, XI, 23-26 (See below, p.251).
      On verso, draft without punctuation of the last two lines of **'To a
      Lady asking Foolish Questions'** [*D*]
b.   **'De Amore'** [*D*], ll.1-14, in purple ink on a page numbered 12.
c.   **'De Amore'** continued, ll.15-32 in purple ink. Numbered 13:
      corrections to l.23 in pencil on back of previous sheet, .
d.   **'De Amore'** concluded, ll.33-52. In purple ink to l.46, then two
      lines in one ink and hand and four in another. Numbered 14.
e.   Ink draft of last stanza of **'Sapientiae Lunae'** [*D*] on page
      numbered 7. On verso, numbered 8A, **'After Paul Verlaine. /
      Spleen'** [*D*] dated 'Feb. 92'.

POÉSIE SCHUBLADE
AND OTHER EARLY POEMS

TO CYNARA

Ah take these songs my love, long time forgiven,
    Songs thou shalt never see,
Yet let them stand as a token that I am shriven,
        As thou by me?

The wrong is old, perchance could I approach thee,
    Eye speak to eye, who knows? —
It should fade as a mist — ah well, I cannot reproach thee —
        He reaps who sows.

Thou loved'st me once and I am still thy lover
        Fain of thee as of old
Fain of thy lips and thy locks that did ever hover
        Twixt brown and gold

Ay woe is me

A MOSAIC

Dreams, dreams of a day gone by!
   (Blue skies and the sunny south)
A fair small face and a rosebud mouth,
   (O Love, my Love and Italy!)
As the moist fresh rain in a time of drouth,
   She came, my Love, as a child to me.

Grey olives and sparkling sea
   Shine bright through the clear calm air —
Of gleaming gold is her waving hair —
   (O Love, my Love and Italy!)
When the world was young and the earth was fair,
   She came, my Love, as a child to me.

Dreams, dreams of a day gone by!
   (Grey eyes and a sunny smile.)
Pure and a maiden and free from guile,
   (O Love, my Love and Italy!)
In a dream she came and a little while
   Tarried and went as a child from me.

White horses out on the sea,
   Mist on the hills and a drizzling rain,
The wind wails loud like a soul in pain: —
   (O Love, my Love and Italy!)
I called her long yet I call in vain,
   Who came and went as a child from me.

REQUIEM

Encircle her head with a clustering wreath
Of lilies and roses and woodland flowers,
That she loved to pluck from garden and heath
When the Earth smelt fresh of sweet May showers,
And no sombre shade of sorrow had laid
A pitiless hand on her sunny hours.

Bring cowslips and violets and redolent may,
And daffodowndillies all yellow clad,
With the pale primrose, but never a spray
Of sorrowing yew or cypress sad
To shadow the grace of her peaceful face,
With aught that is gloomy or dull or grey.

For her life was a garden and she the pale
Queen lily that ruled all that fair emprise.
So weave her of flowers a maiden veil,
That Death may not see her dear grey eyes,
And hold her for aye, in his hut of clay,
Where no sun shines and the stars never rise.

Then one last long kiss on her beautiful hair,
And one last long look at her shapely head, —
Soft — turn away and shed never a tear,
For the purest soul that ever sped,
From a world of dust to her rest we trust —
Nay — what is life that ye weep for the dead?

POTNIA THEA

When the voice of the gods hath spoken,
   The uttered word remains,
The Parcae's web unbroken,
   Its pristine strength retains.

Tho' the Cronian Zeus be dethronèd
   And desolate his shrines,
Anangkè still star-crownèd,
   Her fateful threads entwines.

Tho the goddess, the Cytherean,
   No longer with the Loves
Flits o'er the blue Aegaean
   To hallowed Paphos' groves.

And Athênê has ceased enfolding
   The city of her heart,
Its denizens beholding
   The Delian barque depart,

Still the iconoclastic ages
   Touch not the veilèd dame
Whom husbandmen and sages
   Avouch by different name.

The Olympian queen's forgotten,
　Hephaestus' fires are cold,
The sons of Zeus begotten,
　The heroes rest untold.

Not a sound on the steep Cithaeron,
　Where once the Maenad's choir,
Adored the mighty Bromian,
　With dithyrambic fire.

Still the throne of Anangkè resteth
　Above the reach of years;
Her crape-crowned sceptre breasteth
　The ages without fears.

And when dynasties have been changed
　Of earths and gods and men,
The goddess unestrangèd
　Shall be found ruling then.

RONDEAU

Could you forget, put out of mind,
The vows you made, O most unkind?
The sweet love songs, the fair and frail
Lip utterance without avail,
The pleasure that you used to find,
Or said you found when passion blind,
I kissed the hand that you resigned,
Not all unwilling, maiden pale.
    Tho' you forget!
Where once our sunny paths entwined
There bloweth now the wintry wind: —
Ah dreamt we then time would assail,
Our trust and troth or love could fail,
In those old days that lie behind,
    That you forget?

RONDEAU

In Autumn when the leaf is sere,
In that still season of the year,
Shall we not meet once more we twain,
Who parted in the Spring of pain?
With eyes of passion long grown clear,
When youth is gone and Winter near,
May we not meet once more my dear,
Touch hands, forgive and part again,
  In Autumn?
Tho' bitter anger still doth blear,
The glory of the days that were,
x x
In rare still hours are you not fain
To cry a truce to dear disdain,
  In Autumn?

SONNETS

I.

In Memoriam. H.C. ob. Feb. 24. 1886

I have no heart to wish thee back again
    To this sick earth, poor friend, who may have found,
    Beneath the kind cold shelter of the ground
That calm memorial light that with much pain,
Thou lost in thy last years and sought in vain.
    Nay it is better thus! thy life is crowned
    Tho' but in death with peace — no jarring sound
Shall ever break the sleep wherein thou'rt lain.
Yet when I mournfully recall to mind
    The fragrant summer days I spent with thee
In such calm unison and how thy kind
    Unruffled cheerfulness would oftimes free
My mind from brooding thought I look behind
    And fall before the shrine of memory.

SONNETS

II.

NOVALIS.

"It has grown evening around me while I was looking into the red of
morning."

Novalis.

Ay — even so — fixt was that ardent gaze
    Upon the East — his eagle eyes broad scanned
    The vault of heaven and all the outlying land,
Shadowed in rose and amber neath the rays
Born of the rising sun, — a day of days
    Was dawning for him mystical and grand,
    His budding hopes the morning soft breeze fanned,
The future lay enwrapped in golden haze.
A moment — and the loveliness is gone!
Faded the glamour of morning from his sight,
Faded the quivering radiance that shone
On sea and shore and clothed the hills in light.
A sombre shade of evening settled down
And in the gathering gloom he stood alone.

SONNETS
OF A LITTLE GIRL
(I)

When life doth languish midst the bitter wrong
    That riots everywhere, when all hopes fail,
And comfort is most weak and doubt most strong,
    And friends are false and woman's troth proves frail,
And all thy soul for very life-sickness
    Doth long to end, there yet is one sweet thing,
One fresh oasis in the wilderness
    Of this sad world whereunto thou shalt cling
As to salvation — a child's tender love.
    Ah do not doubt it — all things die and wane,
Save this alone; this only lasts above,
    The lingering rule of weariness and pain,
This love alone is stingless and can calm
Life's fitful fever with its healing balm.

SONNETS
OF A LITTLE GIRL
(II)

Was it at even, with the casement thrown
    Wide to the summer air, I sat and thought,
Of that ideal which I ever sought,
    But fruitlessly — and so was fain to moan —
"Ah weariness of waiting thus alone,
    With vanity of living all distraught,
To find upon the earth nor peace nor aught
    Lovely or pure, whence all things sweet have gone."
And then one passed the dark'ning road along
And lit it with her childhood, that I felt
Passion and bitterness like snowflakes melt
Before the sun, and into praise and song
From the despair wherein it long had dwelt
My life burst flower-like and my soul grew strong.

SONNETS
OF A LITTLE GIRL
(III)

The music in a name, who can conceive,
　　Who may define? Ah child thou dost not know
How many a time when my life's lamp burns low
　　And hope's light flickers—thou wouldst not believe
How thy dear treasured name will oft relieve
　　My sinking heart, how sweetly soft and low
My lips will frame it loath to let it go,
　　And kiss it quietly till I cease to grieve.
It is mine amulet, wrought rich and rare
With lovely fantasies, it is a charm
That whispered gently guardeth me from harm,
It is my ritual, my mystic prayer,
And in the hush of night thro' lattice bars
I see it written in the lonely stars.

SONNETS
OF A LITTLE GIRL
(IV)

Even as a child whose eager fingers snatch
　　An ocean shell and hold it to his ear,
With wondering, awe-struck eyes is hushed to catch
　　The murmurous music of its coilèd sphere;
Whispers of wind and wave, soul-stirring songs
　　Of storm-tossed ships and all the mystery
That to the illimitable sea belongs,
　　Stream to him from its tiny cavity.
As such an one with reverent awe I hold
Thy tender hand, and in those pure grey eyes,
That sweet child face, those tumbled curls of gold,
And in thy smiles and loving, soft replies
　　I find the whole of love, hear full and low
Its mystic ocean's tremulous ebb and flow.

SONNETS
OF A LITTLE GIRL
(V)

When it is over — when the final fight
   Has been out-fought and the last moisty clod
   Rattles upon my coffin, when the sod
Seals me for ever in that land of night
Whence joy and pain have ta'en impartial flight,
   And the old lanes my feet so oft have trod
   Know me no more but all men toil and plod
Over my head, my name forgotten quite.
Wilt thou sometimes — not often — God forfend
That thought of me should chase away thy smile
Or dull thy gladness, yet once in a while
Dream of a day departed and a friend
Who placed above the world and Fortune's prize
The love that centred in thy childish eyes.

[SONNETS
OF A LITTLE GIRL]
(VI)

For the last time, perhaps for weary years
    Perhaps for ever, I have looked upon
    Thy fair fair face; — those grey eyes that have shone
Such comfort on me when the foul fiend fear's
Gaunt haggard laugh would mock me and hot tears
For very loathing of my life rain down,
That trusting smile the one thing sweet I've known
I' the bitterness of life — all disappears.
Farewell, dear saint, I leave thee and I lay
No tax upon thy memory though God knows
This sobbing sea that sadly ebbs and flows
Shall not more surely each returning day
Cling to the callous shore than I in thee
Behold my drear life's dearest memory.

[SONNETS
OF A LITTLE GIRL]
(VII)

So — it is finished and I cannot weep
Nor rave nor utter moan, life is too strong
For my weak will, it carries me along
On its fierce current till I fain would creep
Into some cavern still and fall asleep
And sleeping die, or melt like a sad song
Into the winds — I care not to hold long
This dreary life where pain alone is deep.
O child, my child, forgive me, I am vain,
Unworthy of thy love, I will not task
Even thy pity, who have ta'en a mask
And shall not show my living face again,
Until the end of all things joy and pain
Has given me more than now I dare to ask.

[SONNETS
OF A LITTLE GIRL]
(VIII) EPILOGUE

Let us go hence: the night is now at hand;
The day is overworn, the birds all flown.
And we have reaped the crops the gods have sown;
Despair and death — deep darkness on the land,
Broods for all time; we cannot understand
The meaning of our life, all that is shown
Is bitter to the core, while overthrown
The veil of woe enwraps us where we stand.
Let us go hence, the grave is doubtless cold,
The coffin dark — yet there just and unjust
Find end of labour, there's rest for the old,
Freedom to all from fear and love and lust.
Let us go hence and pray the earth enfold
Our life-sick hearts and turn them into dust.

LA JEUNESSE N'A Q'UN TEMPS

Swiftly passes youth away
Night is coming, fades the day,
All things turn to sombre grey.

Pass the cup and drink, friends, deep
Roses upon roses heap,
Soon it will be time to sleep.

Man, poor man, is born to die,
Love and all things fair will fly
Fill the cup and drain it dry.

Make ye merry, while ye may;
Snatch the sweetness of the day,
Pluck life's pleasures while they stay

When our youth has taken flight,
When the day is lost in night,
There can be no more delight.

Here's a glass to memory
Here's to death and vanity,
Here's a glass to you and me.

SONG OF THE XIXTH CENTURY

O send us light!
More light, more light and fuller clearer day,
We mortals moan and shudder at the night,
And ever still the shadows grow more grey,
    The stars less bright.

O give us faith —
In God, Man, anything to rise and break
The mists of doubt, we cry, but like a wraith
It still eludes our grasp and no rays streak
    The dark of Death.

O give us rest!
We all unrestful sigh, we ask not joy
Who stand with tearless eyes by life opprest, —
Joy turns to pain and love and sorrow cloy,
    But Peace is best.

A LULLABY

Sleep soundly, my pretty child,
   Sleep, sleep on
And all things fearful and all things wild
   Far, far from thy pillow begone,
   Dream of the morrow,
Thou shalt not wake to weep
   Unknowing of sorrow,
O sleep, my little one, dream and sleep.

Sleep softly, my darling sleep!
   Soon, too soon
Dawneth the day when thou canst weep,
Weep, wail for the joy that is flown,
   Wearily yearning,
For love that is passed away,
   For peace unreturning.

SPLEEN

In the dull dark days of our life
  We wander without a goal;
And the plague of living and strife
  Eats worm-like into our soul

To the tune of sighing and tears,
  A weary purposeless band,
For the destined desolate years,
  We fare thro' the Hopeless land.

On our lips are signs as of fire,
  Our eyes are wild with despair,
We are burnt with a fierce desire
  For that we know not nor care.

With loathing of life that is past,
  With horror of days to be,
We shiver like leaves in the blast,
  Neath the breath of memory

In the tearing fangs of remorse
  We are fain to fall in the mire,
And wallowing seek for the source,
  Of the Lethe we desire.

Yet still are we troubled and torn,
By ennui, spleen and regret,
Whatever the depths of our scorn,
We cannot hope to forget.

O man, poor pitiful worm,
Foul nature's filthiest spawn,
As the helmless ship in a storm
So thou from the day thou art born

AFTER MANY YEARS

Sleep on dear now!
    With thy golden hair that flows
On thy calm, thy icy brow
And thy close shut eyes, I trow
The sounds of my song cannot move thee now.
As they moved thee little in life — God knows.

Time was of old,
    I did lull thee on my knee,
And thy locks of rippling gold
Streamed on my arm that did enfold,
And rocked thee to sleep who wast not so cold,
As thou liest now in Death's mystery.

How many years
    Have waned since that distant day,
Seen dim thro' a mist of tears?
How many cycles of years?
Answer me, child, for I have my fears
That it was not real but part of a play.

Is it a dream
    To see thee so calm and cold,
Who when I knew thee did seem
Never more still than the stream?
Or is it part real and partly a dream
Or a dream or in part the days of old?

Have I grown grey?
Or can it be I am dead.
And in spite of all they say,
And all I myself have said,
It is not all done with the very dead,
When the light of this life is worn away?

Nay it is true!
And I cannot doubt dear heart,
That this is really you.
'Tis too sad not to be true
And I mind me now it was this I knew
When the high gods had it that we should part.

You pay no heed,
And I will not linger long
For I trow you have no need
Still to be lulled by my song.
Now you sleep so sound and will sleep so long
You can do without me in very deed.

PRAETERITA

O childish forms and faces
    That live in memorie's shrine;
O pleasant paths and places
    That small feet trod with mine,
The old days that are dying
Soft melodies are sighing
Of something that is lying,
    Pale in the past behind

The laughter that rejoices
    Responds not to our quest,
The tender children's voices,
    Are long time hushed to rest,
And all the stress of ages,
And all the love of sages
Can not return the pages
    That life has once down pressed.

Before us dawns the vista
    Of all our days to be,
But shall we find, my sister,
    The charm that used to be
We know now to our sorrow,
The sad and strange to morrow,
Can never never borrow
    The old time mystery.

When you and I did wander
  On straying childish feet,
Before us lying yonder
  The hills so strange and sweet;
When life was in the dawning,
The fair and golden morning
Sent unto us no warning
  To stay the years' deceit.

The golden light has faded
  That met our dazzled eyes,
The purple hills are shaded,
  And leaden clouds arise;
And spring of childhood's gladness
And youth's brief summer madness
Has yielded to the sadness
  Of dull autumnal skies.

ADIOS!

My sweet child-love, farewell!
   My little tender flower
Who comforted me long and well,
    In many a hope-deserted hour,
     I bid thee now farewell.

The years shall come and go
   And thro' thy village home,
The rippling streamlet still shall flow,
    While far away my footsteps roam,
     Who bid thee now farewell.

O sweet, O saintly face,
   And innocent grey eyes,
That shone with such pathetic grace,
    Wherein such dreamy wisdom lies,
     I bid you now farewell.

Flow on, dear life in peace,
   In peace and purity,
And all my life I shall not cease,
    To hold thee shrined in memory,
     Who bid thee now farewell.

SERAPHITA—SERAPHITUS

I seek for thee, I call thee, O my darling
    In the land of wild unrest,
Very fain I were to see thee and to hold thee
    And be pillowed on thy breast.

All my early hopes and faiths have long time failed me,
    And this life of ours doth seem
In the deathless sleep that hems the world on both sides
    But an evil passing dream

Yet I long for thee, thou one form pure and perfect,
    In the seething obscene throng,
Just to hold thee for one instant and to know thee,
    Then to part and pass along.

It would help me on the dreary path before me,
    On the road thro' Life to Death,
To have met thee once, belovèd, ere I hie me
    To my home the earth beneath.

Somewhere tho' I know thee not, I know thou dwellest,
    Somewhere on the earth, my queen,
Thou art sitting waiting for me fond and faithful,
    Tho' a whole world flow between.

And I send these songs out to thee from the shadows,
    And I call to thee and cling,
Who are shrinèd tho' perchance I never find thee,
    In whatever song I sing.

IT IS FINISHED

The pure grey eyes are closèd now,
    They shall not look on yours again;
Upon that pale and perfect brow,
    There stays no sign of grief or pain.

The little face is white and cold,
    The parted lips give forth no breath,
The grape-like curls of sun-bleached gold,
    Are clammy with the dews of death.

Speak to her and she will not hear,
    Caress her, but she will not move,
No longer feels she hope or fear,
    No longer knows she hate or love.

Ah dream no false or futile dreams,
    Nor lull thyself on fantasy,
That death is other than it seems,
    Or leads to immortality.

She will not speak to thee again,
    Tho' thy whole soul in tears be shed,
For tears and prayers are all in vain,
    She is but dead, she is but dead!

ERE I GO HENCE

Ere I go hence and am no longer seen,
Ere I go hence into the dark of death,
And leave my body and my vital breath,
While over me the grass grows dank and green,
Let me behold thee, let me once again
Press thy fair palm, my fairest without stain,
    Ere I go hence.

Ere I go hence and leave this upper light,
Ere I go hence into the deathless sleep
That lies beyond the land, where cold and deep,
The stream of Lethe flows thro' endless night,
Let me once more, my sweet child love, behold
Thy pure grey eyes, thy tresses of bright gold —
    Ere I go hence.

Ere I go hence and cast away all pain,
Ere I go hence and falter and forget
The fever and the madness and regret
That make all life, all love so passing vain —
O my heart's darling, let me hear once more
The music of thy step upon the floor,
    Ere I go hence.

TRANSIT GLORIA

A gleam thro' the darkness
    Of years and of days,
A transient lifting
    Of misery's haze!

A sound of soft music,
    A momentary lull,
Of this foul gnawing ennui,
    Then all things grow dull.

A rift in life's shadow,
    Brief even as vain,
The madness of pleasure,
    The sadness of pain.

A dream of hope crownèd
    In days of despair;
A vision of beauty
    In Vanity Fair.

Like sweet children's voices,
    To one usèd long,
To harsh-laughing harlots'
    Lascivious song.

Like snow-drops in winter,
   Like soft summer rain,
Like sleep to the weary
   And harassed by pain.

Like long cherished memories,
   Death-white with regret,
Too sad to remember,
   Too sweet to forget.

Dreams of what might have been,
   Ere terrors were rife,
A pause in the passion,
   The fever of life.

A verdant oasis,
   With all around sand,
A gush of blue violets,
   The touch of a hand.

A meeting, a parting,
   For aeons and years;
A smile changing quickly
   To passionate tears.

Ah gone is the phantom
   Of hope and delight,
And faded the vision
   In infinite night.

Life's wave bears me onward
A rudderless bark;
Somewhere in the future,
Death looms in the dark.

The current flows faster,
Loud waileth the wind;
All sweet things and faces
Fade fainter behind.

The end cometh surely,
And each weary wave
Brings nearer and nearer,
The haven, the grave.

And soon from her labour,
Tired mem'ry will cease
And infinite slumber
Bring infinite peace.

'Twas but for a moment
This rift thro' the days,
This transient lifting
Of misery's haze.

SONNET
TO NATURE.

Morituri te salutant.

Thou unclean harpy, odorous of despair,
   I offer up no praises on the shrine
   Of thy wild beauty; thou art not divine,
Nor reverent at all thy tranquil air;
I know thee, evil one, and I am ware
   Of all thy vileness; — never song of mine
   Shall swell the shameful triumphs that are thine
Thou shalt not cajole me of ev'n one prayer.
O false, foul mother who to sate thy lust,
   Insatiate of misery doth consume
The lives that thou hast fashioned out of dust,
   Who feedest on the children of thy womb,
Thy beauty cannot conquer our distrust,
   Thy tenderness is crueller than a tomb.

AWAKENING

We have dreamt dreams but now they are long over,
 Dreams of a life the other side of death;
Drop down the curtain on the play completed,
 The farce of life is finished with the breath.

We have believed the beautiful, false stories,
 Fed on the faiths that after childhood fail,
Now to our eyes the universe appeareth
 A vessel rudderless without a sail.

Man, in a world but fair in semblance only
 Veiling in light its secret of disgust,
Is he not far of all vile things the vilest,
 He, the foul spawn of Nature's filthy lust?

Man with his hopes and pitiful illusions,
 Is he not pitiful, grotesque, forlorn?
White with desire for that life cannot proffer,
 Must we not weep that ever we were born?

Is there one happy? Can there be one happy?
 Nay, for the only good we can attain,
Death our dull goal, the senseless sleep for ever
 Puts alike end to pleasure and to pain.

There shall we rest, but shall not ever know it,
 Shall not have love nor knowledge, nor delight,
Only shall feel the fevered life fall from us,
 Sleepers unwitting in an endless night.

LULLABY

Blow soft thou summer wind,
Rough be not nor unkind,
Whisper outside the room,
Where in the peaceful gloom,
My darling lies a-sleeping.
Let thy soft lullabies
Shut the dear innocent eyes
Of my child who lies a-sleeping.

Stream on ye pale moon-beams,
Light up her childish dreams,
Flow round her small white bed
Halo her golden head —
My darling lies a-sleeping.
Let her repose be sound,
Wrap her in peace around,
My child who lies a-sleeping.

Hush, hush, thou unkind life,
Tumid and full of strife,
Let her sleep tranquilly,
Let her white childhood be,
My sweet who lies a-sleeping.
Save her soft eyes from tears
And the bitter lore of years, —
My child who lies a-sleeping.

THE OLD YEAR

We stand at the end of the old year,
    On the threshold of the new,
And we turn to the old year dying,
    And shrink from the strange and new;
Ah, all fair children, welcome
    The strong, young year that is born,
For us, who are no more children,
    Who have little to do with morn,
We will sit, old year, in the firelight,
    And see the last of you.

There you lie, with your sick, scarred visage,
    Who were once so fair to see,
And the death-dew clings to your forehead,
    And your breath draws painfully: —
In accents low you tell us,
    How there is one end to all,
How love endures for a season,
    How mirth departs in the fall —
As the day is, so the tomorrow,
    As it has been, it shall be.

Where are they, the loves and passions
    Of the old, sad year that dies?
They are dead, they are gone, forgotten
    More swift than the summer skies; —

The tears, the song, the laughter, —
   Ah say, were they worth regret?
Old year, is it kind or cruel,
   That we wander and forget
The good and the ill we gather
   From every year that dies?

Nay we wish thee well, we forgive thee,
   And ywis that this is true, —
There are fairer days in the old years
   Than ever dawn in the new!
What *if* we find fresh faces
   In the young new year that dawns,
A guerdon of joy or sorrow,
   A crown of laurel or thorns, —
There are sweeter things in the old years
   Than ever come with the new.

THE NEW YEAR

The bells ring out, the year is born,
And shall we hope or shall we mourn?
Shall we embrace the young, new year,
Or shall we turn back lingering eyes,
  To the low bier,
Where in his pall the old year lies?

What shall he bring to men who weep,
To men who laugh and men who sleep,
So very weary of the sun?
Shall one of these men ever gain,
  Ah even one,
His heart's desire nor find it vain?

Hope not, fear not: he only bears
The message of the elder years!
A little love, a little pain!
To some a sweet or idle dream,
  To some again,
The sleep wherein we do not dream.

Ah sweet, my child, and yet mine own,
Though I must wander on alone,
Love me a little, clasp me still
With thy soft hands, and I will bear
  For good or ill
The burden of the coming year.

FROM THE ICELANDIC

Long time ago, I vowed to the sea,
    My destined wife,
My one desire, I will give thee my life
    To hold of me:
For others the green, the daedal earth
My joy, my sorrow, my tears, my mirth
    Be thine O sea!

They called me fickle, they called me cold,
    My human loves —
Cried: "His fancy moves as the salt sea moves",
    Who were not told,
How thy bitter kisses held my heart,
Sealed thine forever and set apart
    My bride, my sea!

O changeful one! I cried to the sea,
    O changeless one!
I forget me all things beneath the sun,
    When rocked by thee.
Thine anger woos me, thy tempests thrill,
For am I not thine, to do thy will
    O sea, my sea?

And now thou art risen to prove my vows,
    My wooing done,
I was ever thy lover —, shall I shun
    To be thy spouse?
Was it not this that I knew before,
Waited and yearned for, when I swore
    To wed the sea?

So! — comfort me, cool me, shed thy breath,
    Spare no embrace;
Ah lean thy brow over me, shroud my face,
    Kiss me to Death;
I am one with thee, O most sweet, held fast,
Made thine for ever, thy spouse at last,
    O sea, my sea!

LOVE'S EPILOGUE

When summer dies
    There's an end of singing;
Dumb tears are springing
    To wistful eyes,
At the death of summer
    When the swallow flies,
His swift course winging
    To softer skies.

Ev'n so most sweet,
    Is song time departed,
And we are parted,
    As was most meet,
At the death of summer,
    At the year's defeat,
To cry sad hearted,
    That love is fleet.

Now all is said,
    It were ill to tarry,
With tears to harry,
    Love that is dead.
In the chill of autumn,
    When the leaves are shed,
His corse we carry,
    To earth, his bed.

Ah, look not there,
   To where Love reposes!
Till tired life closes,
   Be fain! Beware!
In the chill of autumn,—
   Ah, forget thee where
With rue and roses,
   Thou hid'st Love's bier

RONDEAU

HÉLÈNE

You loved me once! I charge you, sweet,
Leave me this last, one faith — in spite
Of broken vows and time's deceit,
        You loved me once!
What tho' I sit in utter night
And hear the swift, departing feet
Of young desires that take their flight,
And mourn that love should be so fleet,
And weep that you should prove so light,
The time has been I was complete, —
        You loved me once!

ROUNDEL
TO HÉLÈNE

The golden hours! Ah, prithee, art not fain
Sometimes to drop a tear for their dead sake,
Who were so fair, to yearn for them again,
    The golden hours?
Could I forget them? Not though I should take
Of Lethe and Nepenthe for my pain;
I shall remember, sleeping and awake,
While life is life, my love and thy disdain —
Nay, though I die, methinks, I shall not slake
The thirst wherewith my soul recalls in vain
    The golden hours!

RONDEL

Ah, dear child, in whose kiss
    Is healing of my pain,
Since life has given me this,
    I will no more complain.
My heart to life, ywis,
    Thy clinging hands enchain,
Ah, dear child in whose kiss,
    Is healing of my pain.
Love me — I shall not miss
    Old loves that did but stain,
Thy blue eyes teach me bliss, —
    I am not all in vain,
Ah, dear child, in whose kiss
    Is healing of my pain.

Discedam, explebo numerum, reddarque tenebris,
I decus, i, nostrum; melioribus utere fatis.

Because my life is an unworthy thing
    Outworn and mildewed, I am dismayed,
    I dare not give it thee, O child! O maid!
Too late divined, too sweet for me to sing:
Surely, my barren days I may not bring,
    But rather giftless come, lest any shade
    Or prescience of autumn should be laid
Upon thy fair life in its blossoming.
Yet would I give thee all, who stand aside,
    Giving thee naught: yea! gladly lie down dead
That haply coming, where the roads divide
    On lilies still thy tender feet might tread,
In daisied ways of innocence abide,
    Until thy tale of days is reckoned.

AGAINST MY LADY BURTON: ON HER BURNING THE LAST WRITING OF HER DEAD HUSBAND

"To save his soul", whom narrowly she loved
She did this deed of everlasting shame,
For devils' laughter; and was soulless proved
Heaping dishonour on her scholar's name.
Her lean distrust awoke when he was dead;
Dead, hardly cold; whose life was worn away
In scholarship's high service; from his head
She lightly tore his ultimate crown of bay.
His masterpiece, the ripe fruit of his age,
In art's despite she gave the hungry flame;
Smiled at the death of each laborious page,
Which she read only by the light of shame.
Dying he trusted her: him dead she paid
Most womanly, destroying his life's prize:
So Judas decently his Lord betrayed
With deep dishonour wrought in love's disguise.
With deep dishonour, for her jealous heart
His whole life's work, with light excuse put by
For love of him, or haply, hating art.
Oh Love be this, let us curse Love and die.
Nay! Love forgive: could such a craven thing
Love anywhere? but let her name pass down
Dishonoured through the ages, who did fling
To the rank scented mob a sage's crown,
And offered Fame, Love, Honour, mincingly
To her one God — sterile Propriety!

EARLY AND UNCOLLECTED POEMS

A LETTER FROM M.M. VERSIFIED OUT OF POOR PROSE INTO CATCHPENNY VERSE!

Dear Sir! would you be popular,
    Then never mention Greek!
Be arrogant and insular,
    Dear Sir, would you be popular:
Cut classics; and for guiding star,
Read Birrell once a week.
Dear Sir! would you be popular,
    Then never mention Greek.

Lionel Johnson.

FRAGMENT

In the days of the good, gay people,
Of the little folk in green,
The Moon shone clear in Fairyland,
Or ever the world was seen.

THE PASSING OF TENNYSON

As his own Arthur fared across the mere,
With the grave Queen, past knowledge of the throng,
Serene and calm, rebuking grief and tear,
Departs this prince of song.

Whom the gods love Death doth not cleave nor smite,
But like an angel, with soft trailing wing,
He gathers them upon the hush of night,
With voice and beckoning.

The moonlight falling on that august head
Smoothed out the mark of time's defiling hand,
And hushed the voice of mourning round his bed—
'He goes to his own land'.

Beyond the ramparts of the world where stray
The laureled few o'er fields Elysian,
He joins his elders of the lyre and bay,
Led by the Mantuan.

We mourn him not, but sigh with Bedivere,
Not perished be the sword he bore so long,
Excalibur, whom none is left to wear—
His magic brand of song.

FANTAISIE TRISTE

To my first love,
    Loved all above;
  I'the late spring,
    Pansies, pansies,
    Such strange fancies,
Were all I had to bring.

To my last love,
    Loved all above;
  At evening,
  One chrysanthemum
    Of wan autumn
Is all I have to bring.

  In a dim past,
    Overcast
With the dead flow'rs
    And the strayed hours;
(There are no flowers left to bring,
There are no songs left to sing)
    Let first be last!

VERSES

Vitae summa brevis spem nos vetat incohare longam.

They are not long, the weeping and the laughter,
  Love and desire and hate:
I think they have no portion in us after
  We pass the gate.

They are not long, the days of wine and roses:
  Out of a misty dream
Our path emerges for a while, then closes
  Within a dream.

IN PREFACE: FOR ADELAIDE.

To you, who are my verses, as on some very future day, if you ever care to read them, you will understand, would it not be somewhat trivial to dedicate any one verse, as I may do, in all humility, to my friends? Trivial, too, perhaps, only to name you even here? Trivial, presumptuous? For I need not write your name for you at least to know that this and all my work is made for you in the first place, and I need not to be reminded by my critics that I have no silver tongue such as were fit to praise you. So for once you shall go indedicate, if not quite anonymous; and I will only commend my little book to you in sentences far beyond my poor compass which will help you perhaps to be kind to it:

'Votre personne, vos moindres mouvements me semblaient avoir dans le monde une importance extra-humaine. Mon coeur comme de la poussière se soulevait derrière vos pas. Vous me faisiez l'effet d'un clair-de-lune par une nuit d'été, quand tout est parfums, ombres douces, blancheurs, infini; et les délices de la chair et de l'âme étaient contenues pour moi dans votre nom que je me répétais en tachant de le baiser sur mes lèvres.

'Quelquefois vos paroles me reviennent comme un écho lointain, comme le son d'une cloche apporté par le vent; et il me semble que vous êtes là quand je lis des passages de l'amour dans les livres.... Tout ce qu'on y blâme d'exagéré, vous me l'avez fait ressentir.'

PONT-AVEN, FINISTÈRE, 1896.

A CORONAL
With His songs and Her days to His Lady and to Love.

Violets and leaves of vine,
    Into a frail, fair wreath
We gather and entwine:
    A wreath for Love to wear,
    Fragrant as his own breath,
To crown his brow divine,
    All day till night is near.
Violets and leaves of vine
We gather and entwine.

Violets and leaves of vine
    For Love that lives a day,
We gather and entwine.
    All day till Love is dead,
    Till eve falls, cold and gray,
These blossoms, yours and mine,
    Love wears upon his head.
Violets and leaves of vine
We gather and entwine.

Violets and leaves of vine,
    For Love when poor Love dies
We gather and entwine.
    This wreath that lives a day
    Over his pale, cold eyes,
Kissed shut by Proserpine,
    At set of sun we lay:
Violets and leaves of vine
We gather and entwine.

VERSES.

NUNS OF THE PERPETUAL ADORATION.
For THE COUNTESS SOBIESKA VON PLATT.

Calm, sad, secure; behind high convent walls,
    These watch the sacred lamp, these watch and pray:
And it is one with them when evening falls,
    And one with them the cold return of day.

These heed not time; their nights and days they make
    Into a long, returning rosary,
Whereon their lives are threaded for Christ's sake:
    Meekness and vigilance and chastity.

A vowed patrol, in silent companies,
    Life-long they keep before the living Christ:
In the dim church, their prayers and penances
    Are fragrant incense to the Sacrificed.

Outside, the world is wild and passionate;
    Man's weary laughter and his sick despair
Entreat at their impenetrable gate:
    They heed no voices in their dream of prayer.

They saw the glory of the world displayed;
    They saw the bitter of it, and the sweet;
They knew the roses of the world should fade,
    And be trod under by the hurrying feet.

Therefore they rather put away desire,
    And crossed their hands and came to sanctuary;
And veiled their heads and put on coarse attire:
    Because their comeliness was vanity.

And there they rest; they have serene insight
    Of the illuminating dawn to be:
Mary's sweet Star dispels for them the night,
    The proper darkness of humanity.

Calm, sad, secure; with faces worn and mild:
    Surely their choice of vigil is the best?
Yea! for our roses fade, the world is wild;
    But there, beside the altar, there, is rest.

VILLANELLE OF SUNSET.

Come hither, Child! and rest:
This is the end of day,
Behold the weary West!

Sleep rounds with equal zest
Man's toil and children's play:
Come hither, Child! and rest.

My white bird, seek thy nest,
Thy drooping head down lay:
Behold the weary West!

Now are the flowers confest
Of slumber: sleep, as they!
Come hither, Child! and rest.

Now eve is manifest,
And homeward lies our way:
Behold the weary West!

Tired flower! upon my breast,
I would wear thee alway:
Come hither, Child! and rest;
Behold, the weary West!

MY LADY APRIL.

For LÉOPOLD NELKEN.

Dew on her robe and on her tangled hair;
  Twin dewdrops for her eyes; behold her pass,
  With dainty step brushing the young, green grass,
The while she trills some high, fantastic air,
Full of all feathered sweetness: she is fair,
  And all her flower-like beauty, as a glass,
  Mirrors out hope and love: and still, alas!
Traces of tears her languid lashes wear.

Say, doth she weep for very wantonness?
  Or is it that she dimly doth foresee
Across her youth the joys grow less and less,
  The burden of the days that are to be:
  Autumn and withered leaves and vanity,
And winter bringing end in barrenness.

TO ONE IN BEDLAM.

For HENRY DAVRAY.

With delicate, mad hands, behind his sordid bars,
Surely he hath his posies, which they tear and twine;
Those scentless wisps of straw, that miserably line
His strait, caged universe, whereat the dull world stares,

Pedant and pitiful. O, how his rapt gaze wars
With their stupidity! Know they what dreams divine
Lift his long, laughing reveries like enchaunted wine,
And make his melancholy germane to the stars'?

O lamentable brother! if those pity thee,
Am I not fain of all thy lone eyes promise me;
Half a fool's kingdom, far from men who sow and reap,
All their days, vanity? Better than mortal flowers,
Thy moon-kissed roses seem: better than love or sleep,
The star-crowned solitude of thine oblivious hours!

AD DOMNULAM SUAM.

Little lady of my heart!
  Just a little longer,
Love me: we will pass and part,
  Ere this love grow stronger.

I have loved thee, Child! too well,
  To do aught but leave thee:
Nay! my lips should never tell
  Any tale, to grieve thee.

Little lady of my heart!
  Just a little longer,
I may love thee: we will part,
  Ere my love grow stronger.

Soon thou leavest fairy-land;
  Darker grow thy tresses:
Soon no more of hand in hand;
  Soon no more caresses!

Little lady of my heart!
  Just a little longer,
Be a child: then, we will part,
  Ere this love grow stronger.

AMOR UMBRATILIS.

A gift of Silence, sweet!
  Who may not ever hear:
To lay down at your unobservant feet,
  Is all the gift I bear.

I have no songs to sing,
  That you should heed or know:
I have no lilies, in full hands, to fling
  Across the path you go.

I cast my flowers away,
  Blossoms unmeet for you!
The garland I have gathered in my day:
  My rosemary and rue.

I watch you pass and pass,
  Serene and cold: I lay
My lips upon your trodden, daisied grass,
  And turn my life away.

Yea, for I cast you, sweet!
  This one gift, you shall take:
Like ointment, on your unobservant feet,
  My silence, for your sake.

AMOR PROFANUS.

For GABRIEL DE LAUTREC.

Beyond the pale of memory,
In some mysterious dusky grove;
A place of shadows utterly,
Where never coos the turtle-dove,
A world forgotten of the sun:
I dreamed we met when day was done,
And marvelled at our ancient love.

Met there by chance, long kept apart,
We wandered, through the darkling glades;
And that old language of the heart
We sought to speak: alas! poor shades!
Over our pallid lips had run
The waters of oblivion,
Which crown all loves of men or maids.

In vain we stammered: from afar
Our old desire shone cold and dead:
That time was distant as a star,
When eyes were bright and lips were red.
And still we went with downcast eye
And no delight in being nigh,
Poor shadows most uncomforted.

Ah, Lalage! while life is ours,
Hoard not thy beauty rose and white,
But pluck the pretty, fleeting flowers
That deck our little path of light:
For all too soon we twain shall tread
The bitter pastures of the dead:
Estranged, sad spectres of the night.

VILLANELLE OF MARGUERITES.

For Miss Eugénie Magnus.

'A little, passionately, not at all?'
She casts the snowy petals on the air:
And what care we how many petals fall!

Nay, wherefore seek the seasons to forestall?
It is but playing, and she will not care,
A little, passionately, not at all!

She would not answer us if we should call
Across the years: her visions are too fair;
And what care we how many petals fall!

She knows us not, nor recks if she enthrall
With voice and eyes and fashion of her hair,
A little, passionately, not at all!

Knee-deep she goes in meadow grasses tall,
Kissed by the daisies that her fingers tear:
And what care we how many petals fall!

We pass and go: but she shall not recall
What men we were, nor all she made us bear:
'A little, passionately, not at all!'
And what care we how many petals fall!

YVONNE OF BRITTANY.

For MARMADUKE LANGDALE.

In your mother's apple-orchard,
  Just a year ago, last spring:
Do you remember, Yvonne!
    The dear trees lavishing
Rain of their starry blossoms
    To make you a coronet?
Do you ever remember, Yvonne?
    As I remember yet.

In your mother's apple-orchard,
    When the world was left behind:
You were shy, so shy, Yvonne!
    But your eyes were calm and kind.
We spoke of the apple harvest,
    When the cider press is set,
And such-like trifles, Yvonne!
    That doubtless you forget.

In the still, soft Breton twilight,
    We were silent; words were few,
Till your mother came out chiding,
    For the grass was bright with dew:
But I know your heart was beating,
    Like a fluttered, frightened dove.
Do you ever remember, Yvonne?
    That first faint flush of love?

In the fulness of midsummer,
     When the apple-bloom was shed,
Oh, brave was your surrender,
     Though shy the words you said.
I was glad, so glad, Yvonne!
     To have led you home at last;
Do you ever remember, Yvonne!
     How swiftly the days passed?

In your mother's apple-orchard
     It is grown too dark to stray,
There is none to chide you, Yvonne!
     You are over far away.
There is dew on your grave grass, Yvonne!
     But your feet it shall not wet:
No, you never remember, Yvonne!
     And I shall soon forget.

BENEDICTIO DOMINI.

For SELWYN IMAGE

Without, the sullen noises of the street!
The voice of London, inarticulate,
Hoarse and blaspheming, surges in to meet
The silent blessing of the Immaculate.

Dark is the church, and dim the worshippers,
Hushed with bowed heads as though by some old spell,
While through the incense-laden air there stirs
The admonition of a silver bell.

Dark is the church, save where the altar stands,
Dressed like a bride, illustrious with light,
Where one old priest exalts with tremulous hands
The one true solace of man's fallen plight.

Strange silence here: without, the sounding street
Heralds the world's swift passage to the fire:
O Benediction, perfect and complete!
When shall men cease to suffer and desire?

GROWTH.

I watched the glory of her childhood change,
Half-sorrowful to find the child I knew,
(Loved long ago in lily-time)
Become a maid, mysterious and strange,
With fair, pure eyes — dear eyes, but not the eyes I knew
Of old, in the olden time!

Till on my doubting soul the ancient good
Of her dear childhood in the new disguise
Dawned, and I hastened to adore
The glory of her waking maidenhood,
And found the old tenderness within her deepening eyes,
But kinder than before.

AD MANUS PUELLAE.

For Leonard Smithers.

I was always a lover of ladies' hands!
    Or ever mine heart came here to tryst,
For the sake of your carved white hands' commands;
    The tapering fingers, the dainty wrist;
    The hands of a girl were what I kissed.

I remember an hand like a *fleur-de-lys*
    When it slid from its silken sheath, her glove;
With its odours passing ambergris:
    And that was the empty husk of a love.
    Oh, how shall I kiss your hands enough?

They are pale with the pallor of ivories;
    But they blush to the tips like a curled sea-shell:
What treasure, in kingly treasuries,
    Of gold, and spice for the thurible,
    Is sweet as her hands to hoard and tell?

I know not the way from your finger-tips,
    Nor how I shall gain the higher lands,
The citadel of your sacred lips:
    I am captive still of my pleasant bands,
    The hands of a girl, and most your hands.

FLOS LUNAE.

For YVANHOÉ RAMBOSSON.

I would not alter thy cold eyes,
Nor trouble the calm fount of speech
With aught of passion or surprise.
The heart of thee I cannot reach:
I would not alter thy cold eyes!

I would not alter thy cold eyes;
Nor have thee smile, nor make thee weep:
Though all my life droops down and dies,
Desiring thee, desiring sleep,
I would not alter thy cold eyes.

I would not alter thy cold eyes;
I would not change thee if I might,
To whom my prayers for incense rise,
Daughter of dreams! my moon of night!
I would not alter thy cold eyes.

I would not alter thy cold eyes,
With trouble of the human heart:
Within their glance my spirit lies,
A frozen thing, alone, apart;
I would not alter thy cold eyes.

NON SUM QUALIS ERAM BONAE SUB REGNO CYNARAE.

Last night, ah, yesternight, betwixt her lips and mine
There fell thy shadow, Cynara! thy breath was shed
Upon my soul between the kisses and the wine;
And I was desolate and sick of an old passion,
    Yea, I was desolate and bowed my head:
I have been faithful to thee, Cynara! in my fashion.

All night upon mine heart I felt her warm heart beat,
Night-long within mine arms in love and sleep she lay;
Surely the kisses of her bought red mouth were sweet;
But I was desolate and sick of an old passion,
    When I awoke and found the dawn was gray:
I have been faithful to thee, Cynara! in my fashion.

I have forgot much, Cynara! gone with the wind,
Flung roses, roses riotously with the throng,
Dancing, to put thy pale, lost lilies out of mind;
But I was desolate and sick of an old passion,
    Yea, all the time, because the dance was long:
I have been faithful to thee, Cynara! in my fashion.

I cried for madder music and for stronger wine,
But when the feast is finished and the lamps expire,
Then falls thy shadow, Cynara! the night is thine;
And I am desolate and sick of an old passion,
    Yea hungry for the lips of my desire:
I have been faithful to thee, Cynara! in my fashion.

VANITAS.

For VINCENT O'SULLIVAN.

Beyond the need of weeping,
    Beyond the reach of hands,
May she be quietly sleeping,
    In what dim nebulous lands?
Ah, she who understands!

The long, long winter weather,
    These many years and days,
Since she, and Death, together,
    Left me the wearier ways:
And now, these tardy bays!

The crown and victor's token:
    How are they worth to-day?
The one word left unspoken,
    It were late now to say:
But cast the palm away!

For once, ah once, to meet her,
    Drop laurel from tired hands:
Her cypress were the sweeter,
    In her oblivious lands:
Haply she understands!

Yet, crossed that weary river,
    In some ulterior land,
Or anywhere, or ever,
    Will she stretch out a hand?
And will she understand?

EXILE.

For CONAL HOLMES O'CONNELL O'RIORDAN.

By the sad waters of separation
Where we have wandered by divers ways,
I have but the shadow and imitation
Of the old memorial days.

In music I have no consolation,
No roses are pale enough for me;
The sound of the waters of separation
Surpasseth roses and melody.

By the sad waters of separation
Dimly I hear from an hidden place
The sigh of mine ancient adoration:
Hardly can I remember your face.

If you be dead, no proclamation
Sprang to me over the waste, gray sea:
Living, the waters of separation
Sever for ever your soul from me.

No man knoweth our desolation;
Memory pales of the old delight;
While the sad waters of separation
Bear us on to the ultimate night.

SPLEEN.

For ARTHUR SYMONS.

I was not sorrowful, I could not weep,
And all my memories were put to sleep.

I watched the river grow more white and strange,
All day till evening I watched it change.

All day till evening I watched the rain
Beat wearily upon the window pane.

I was not sorrowful, but only tired
Of everything that ever I desired.

Her lips, her eyes, all day became to me
The shadow of a shadow utterly.

All day mine hunger for her heart became
Oblivion, until the evening came,

And left me sorrowful, inclined to weep,
With all my memories that could not sleep.

O MORS! QUAM AMARA EST MEMORIA TUA
HOMINI PACEM HABENTI IN SUBSTANTIIS SUIS.

Exceeding sorrow
   Consumeth my sad heart!
Because to-morrow
   We must depart,
Now is exceeding sorrow
   All my part!

Give over playing,
   Cast thy viol away:
Merely laying
   Thine head my way:
Prithee, give over playing,
   Grave or gay.

Be no word spoken;
   Weep nothing: let a pale
Silence, unbroken
   Silence prevail!
Prithee, be no word spoken,
   Lest I fail!

Forget to-morrow!
   Weep nothing: only lay
In silent sorrow
   Thine head my way:
Let us forget to-morrow,
   This one day!

> *Ah, dans ces mornes séjours*
> *Les jamais sont les toujours.*
>
> PAUL VERLAINE.

You would have understood me, had you waited;
    I could have loved you, dear! as well as he:
Had we not been impatient, dear! and fated
        Always to disagree.

What is the use of speech? Silence were fitter:
    Lest we should still be wishing things unsaid.
Though all the words we ever spake were bitter,
        Shall I reproach you dead?

Nay, let this earth, your portion, likewise cover
    All the old anger, setting us apart:
Always, in all, in truth was I your lover;
        Always, I held your heart.

I have met other women who were tender,
    As you were cold, dear! with a grace as rare.
Think you, I turned to them, or made surrender,
        I who had found you fair?

Had we been patient, dear! ah, had you waited,
    I had fought death for you, better than he:
But from the very first, dear! we were fated
        Always to disagree.

Late, late, I come to you, now death discloses
    Love that in life was not to be our part:
On your low lying mound between the roses,
    Sadly I cast my heart.

I would not waken you: nay! this is fitter;
    Death and the darkness give you unto me;
Here we who loved so, were so cold and bitter,
    Hardly can disagree.

APRIL LOVE.

For ARTHUR CECIL HILLIER.

We have walked in Love's land a little way,
    We have learnt his lesson a little while,
And shall we not part at the end of day,
    With a sigh, a smile?

A little while in the shine of the sun,
    We were twined together, joined lips, forgot
How the shadows fall when the day is done,
    And when Love is not.

We have made no vows — there will none be broke,
    Our love was free as the wind on the hill,
There was no word said we need wish unspoke,
    We have wrought no ill.

So shall we not part at the end of day,
    Who have loved and lingered a little while,
Join lips for the last time, go our way,
    With a sigh, a smile?

VAIN HOPE.

Sometimes, to solace my sad heart, I say,
　Though late it be, though lily-time be past,
　Though all the summer skies be overcast,
Haply I will go down to her, some day,
　And cast my rests of life before her feet,
That she may have her will of me, being so sweet,
　And none gainsay!

So might she look on me with pitying eyes,
　And lay calm hands of healing on my head:
　'Because of thy long pains be comforted;
For I, even I, am Love: sad soul, arise!'
　So, for her graciousness, I might at last
Gaze on the very face of Love, and hold Him fast
　In no disguise.

Haply, I said, she will take pity on me,
　Though late I come, long after lily-time,
　With burden of waste days and drifted rhyme:
Her kind, calm eyes, down drooping maidenly,
　Shall change, grow soft: there yet is time, meseems,
I said, for solace; though I know these things are dreams
　And may not be!

93

VAIN RESOLVES.

I said: 'There is an end of my desire:
    Now have I sown, and I have harvested,
And these are ashes of an ancient fire,
    Which, verily, shall not be quickened.
Now will I take me to a place of peace,
    Forget mine heart's desire;
In solitude and prayer, work out my soul's release.

'I shall forget her eyes, how cold they were;
    Forget her voice, how soft it was and low,
With all my singing that she did not hear,
    And all my service that she did not know.
I shall not hold the merest memory
    Of any days that were,
Within those solitudes where I will fasten me.'

And once she passed, and once she raised her eyes,
    And smiled for courtesy, and nothing said:
And suddenly the old flame did uprise,
    And all my dead desire was quickened.
Yea! as it hath been, it shall ever be,
    Most passionless, pure eyes!
Which never shall grow soft, nor change, nor pity me.

A REQUIEM.

For JOHN GRAY.

Neobule, being tired,
Far too tired to laugh or weep,
From the hours, rosy and gray,
Hid her golden face away.
Neobule, fain of sleep,
Slept at last as she desired!

Neobule! is it well,
That you haunt the hollow lands,
Where the poor, dead people stray,
Ghostly, pitiful and gray,
Plucking, with their spectral hands,
Scentless blooms of asphodel?

Neobule, tired to death
Of the flowers that I threw
On her flower-like, fair feet,
Sighed for blossoms not so sweet,
Lunar roses pale and blue,
Lilies of the world beneath.

Neobule! ah, too tired
Of the dreams and days above!
Where the poor, dead people stray,
Ghostly, pitiful and gray,
Out of life and out of love,
Sleeps the sleep which she desired.

BEATA SOLITUDO.

For SAM. SMITH.

What land of Silence,
　　Where pale stars shine
On apple-blossom
　　And dew-drenched vine,
　　Is yours and mine?

The silent valley
　　That we will find,
Where all the voices
　　Of humankind
　　Are left behind.

There all forgetting,
　　Forgotten quite,
We will repose us,
　　With our delight
　　Hid out of sight.

The world forsaken,
　　And out of mind
Honour and labour,
　　We shall not find
　　The stars unkind.

And men shall travail,
    And laugh and weep;
But we have vistas
    Of gods asleep,
    With dreams as deep.

A land of Silence,
    Where pale stars shine
On apple-blossoms
    And dew-drenched vine,
    Be yours and mine!

TERRE PROMISE.

For HERBERT P. HORNE.

Even now the fragrant darkness of her hair
Had brushed my cheek; and once, in passing by,
Her hand upon my hand lay tranquilly:
What things unspoken trembled in the air!

Always I know, how little severs me
From mine heart's country, that is yet so far;
And must I lean and long across a bar,
That half a word would shatter utterly?

Ah might it be, that just by touch of hand,
Or speaking silence, shall the barrier fall;
And she shall pass, with no vain words at all,
But droop into mine arms, and understand!

AUTUMNAL.

For ALEXANDER TEIXEIRA DE MATTOS.

Pale amber sunlight falls across
   The reddening October trees,
   That hardly sway before a breeze
As soft as summer: summer's loss
   Seems little, dear! on days like these!

Let misty autumn be our part!
   The twilight of the year is sweet:
   Where shadow and the darkness meet
Our love, a twilight of the heart
   Eludes a little time's deceit.

Are we not better and at home
   In dreamful Autumn, we who deem
   No harvest joy is worth a dream?
A little while and night shall come,
   A little while, then, let us dream.

Beyond the pearled horizons lie
   Winter and night: awaiting these
   We garner this poor hour of ease,
Until love turn from us and die
   Beneath the drear November trees.

IN TEMPORE SENECTUTIS.

When I am old,
  And sadly steal apart,
Into the dark and cold,
  Friend of my heart!
Remember, if you can,
Not him who lingers, but that other man,
Who loved and sang, and had a beating heart, —
  When I am old!

When I am old,
  And all Love's ancient fire
Be tremulous and cold:
  My soul's desire!
Remember, if you may,
Nothing of you and me but yesterday,
When heart on heart we bid the years conspire
  To make us old.

When I am old,
  And every star above
Be pitiless and cold:
  My life's one love!
Forbid me not to go:
Remember nought of us but long ago,
And not at last, how love and pity strove
  When I grew old!

VILLANELLE OF HIS LADY'S TREASURES.

I took her dainty eyes, as well
   As silken tendrils of her hair:
And so I made a Villanelle!

I took her voice, a silver bell,
   As clear as song, as soft as prayer;
I took her dainty eyes as well.

It may be, said I, who can tell,
   These things shall be my less despair?
And so I made a Villanelle!

I took her whiteness virginal
   And from her cheek two roses rare:
I took her dainty eyes as well.

I said: 'It may be possible
   Her image from my heart to tear!'
And so I made a Villanelle.

I stole her laugh, most musical:
   I wrought it in with artful care;
I took her dainty eyes as well;
And so I made a Villanelle.

GRAY NIGHTS.

For CHARLES SAYLE.

Awhile we wandered (thus it is I dream!)
Through a long, sandy tract of No Man's Land,
Where only poppies grew among the sand,
The which we, plucking, cast with scant esteem,
And ever sadlier, into the sad stream,
Which followed us, as we went, hand in hand,
Under the estrangèd stars, a road unplanned,
Seeing all things in the shadow of a dream.

And ever sadlier, as the stars expired,
We found the poppies rarer, till thine eyes
Grown all my light, to light me were too tired,
And at their darkening, that no surmise
Might haunt me of the lost days we desired,
After them all I flung those memories!

VESPERAL.

For HUBERT CRACKANTHORPE.

Strange grows the river on the sunless evenings!
The river comforts me, grown spectral, vague and dumb:
Long was the day; at last the consoling shadows come:
Sufficient for the day are the day's evil things!

Labour and longing and despair the long day brings;
Patient till evening men watch the sun go west;
Deferred, expected night at last brings sleep and rest:
Sufficient for the day are the day's evil things!

At last the tranquil Angelus of evening rings
Night's curtain down for comfort and oblivion
Of all the vanities observèd by the sun:
Sufficient for the day are the day's evil things!

So, some time, when the last of all our evenings
Crowneth memorially the last of all our days,
Not loth to take his poppies man goes down and says,
'Sufficient for the day were the day's evil things!'

THE GARDEN OF SHADOW.

Love heeds no more the sighing of the wind
Against the perfect flowers: thy garden's close
Is grown a wilderness, where none shall find
One strayed, last petal of one last year's rose.

O bright, bright hair! O mouth like a ripe fruit!
Can famine be so nigh to harvesting?
Love, that was songful, with a broken lute
In grass of graveyards goeth murmuring.

Let the wind blow against the perfect flowers,
And all thy garden change and glow with spring:
Love is grown blind with no more count of hours,
Nor part in seed-time nor in harvesting.

SOLI CANTARE PERITI ARCADES.

For AUBREY BEARDSLEY.

Oh, I would live in a dairy,
    And its Colin I would be,
And many a rustic fairy
    Should churn the milk with me.

Or the fields should be my pleasure,
    And my flocks should follow me,
Piping a frolic measure
    For Joan or Marjorie.

For the town is black and weary,
    And I hate the London street;
But the country ways are cheery,
    And country lanes are sweet.

Good luck to you, Paris ladies!
    Ye are over fine and nice,
I know where the country maid is,
    Who needs not asking twice.

Ye are brave in your silks and satins,
    As ye mince about the Town;
But her feet go free in pattens,
    If she wear a russet gown.

If she be not queen nor goddess
　　She shall milk my brown-eyed herds,
And the breasts beneath her boddice
　　Are whiter than her curds.

So I will live in a dairy,
　　And its Colin I will be,
And it's Joan that I will marry,
　　Or, haply, Marjorie.

ON THE BIRTH OF A FRIEND'S CHILD

For VICTOR AND NELLIE PLARR.

Mark the day white, on which the Fates have smiled:
Eugenio and Egeria have a child.
On whom abundant grace kind Jove imparts
If she but copy either parent's parts.
Then, Muses! long devoted to her race,
Grant her Egeria's virtues and her face;
Nor stop your bounty there, but add to it
Eugenio's learning and Eugenio's wit.

EXTREME UNCTION.

For LIONEL JOHNSON.

Upon the eyes, the lips, the feet,
    On all the passages of sense,
The atoning oil is spread with sweet
    Renewal of lost innocence.

The feet, that lately ran so fast
    To meet desire, are soothly sealed;
The eyes, that were so often cast
    On vanity, are touched and healed.

From troublous sights and sounds set free;
    In such a twilight hour of breath,
Shall one retrace his life, or see,
    Through shadows, the true face of death?

Vials of mercy! Sacring oils!
    I know not where nor when I come,
Nor through what wanderings and toils,
    To crave of you Viaticum.

Yet, when the walls of flesh grow weak,
    In such an hour, it well may be,
Through mist and darkness, light will break,
    And each anointed sense will see.

AMANTIUM IRAE.

When this, our rose, is faded,
   And these, our days, are done,
In lands profoundly shaded
   From tempest and from sun:
Ah, once more come together,
   Shall we forgive the past,
And safe from worldly weather
   Possess our souls at last?

Or in our place of shadows
   Shall still we stretch an hand
To green, remembered meadows,
   Of that old pleasant land?
And vainly there foregathered,
   Shall we regret the sun?
The rose of love, ungathered?
   The bay, we have not won?

Ah, child! the world's dark marges
   May lead to Nevermore,
The stately funeral barges
   Sail for an unknown shore,
And love we vow to-morrow,
   And pride we serve to-day:
What if they both should borrow
   Sad hues of yesterday?

Our pride! Ah, should we miss it,
   Or will it serve at last?
Our anger, if we kiss it,
   Is like a sorrow past.
While roses deck the garden,
   While yet the sun is high,
Doff sorry pride for pardon,
   Or ever love go by.

IMPENITENTIA ULTIMA.

For ROBERT HARBOROUGH SHERARD.

Before my light goes out for ever if God should give me a choice of
  graces,
  I would not reck of length of days, nor crave for things to be;
But cry: 'One day of the great lost days, one face of all the faces,
  Grant me to see and touch once more and nothing more to see.

'For, Lord, I was free of all Thy flowers, but I chose the world's sad
  roses,
  And that is why my feet are torn and mine eyes are blind with
  sweat,
But at Thy terrible judgement-seat, when this my tired life closes,
  I am ready to reap whereof I sowed, and pay my righteous debt.

'But once before the sand is run and the silver thread is broken,
  Give me a grace and cast aside the veil of dolorous years,
Grant me one hour of all mine hours, and let me see for a token
  Her pure and pitiful eyes shine out, and bathe her feet with tears.'

Her pitiful hands should calm, and her hair stream down and blind
  me,
  Out of the sight of night, and out of the reach of fear,
And her eyes should be my light whilst the sun went out behind me,
  And the viols in her voice be the last sound in mine ear.

Before the ruining waters fall and my life be carried under,
  And Thine anger cleave me through as a child cuts down a flower,
I will praise Thee, Lord, in Hell, while my limbs are racked asunder,
  For the last sad sight of her face and the little grace of an hour.

111

A VALEDICTION.

If we must part,
    Then let it be like this;
Not heart on heart,
    Nor with the useless anguish of a kiss;
But touch mine hand and say:
'Until to-morrow or some other day,
    If we must part.'

Words are so weak
    When love hath been so strong:
Let silence speak:
    'Life is a little while, and love is long;
A time to sow and reap,
And after harvest a long time to sleep,
    But words are weak.'

SAPIENTIA LUNAE.

For ANDRÉ LEBEY.

The wisdom of the world said unto me:
   'Go forth and run, the race is to the brave;
Perchance some honour tarrieth for thee!'
     'As tarrieth,' I said, 'for sure, the grave.'
       For I had pondered on a rune of roses,
       Which to her votaries the moon discloses.

The wisdom of the world said: *'There are bays:*
   Go forth and run, for victory is good,
After the stress of the laborious days.'
     'Yet,' said I, 'shall I be the worms' sweet food,'
       As I went musing on a rune of roses,
       Which in her hour, the pale, soft moon discloses.

Then said my voices: *'Wherefore strive or run,*
   On dusty highways ever, a vain race?
The long night cometh, starless, void of sun,
     What light shall serve thee like her golden face?'
       For I had pondered on a rune of roses,
       And knew some secrets which the moon discloses.

'Yea,' said I, 'for her eyes are pure and sweet
   As lilies, and the fragrance of her hair
Is many laurels; and it is not meet
     To run for shadows when the prize is here;'
       And I went reading in that rune of roses
       Which to her votaries the moon discloses.

Dum nos fata sinunt, oculos satiemus Amore.

PROPERTIUS.

Cease smiling, Dear! a little while be sad,
    Here in the silence, under the wan moon;
Sweet are thine eyes, but how can I be glad,
    Knowing they change so soon?

For Love's sake, Dear, be silent! Cover me
    In the deep darkness of thy falling hair:
Fear is upon me and the memory
    Of what is all men's share.

O could this moment be perpetuate!
    Must we grow old, and leaden-eyed and gray,
And taste no more the wild and passionate
    Love sorrows of to-day?

Grown old, and faded, Sweet! and past desire,
    Let memory die, lest there be too much ruth,
Remembering the old, extinguished fire
    Of our divine, lost youth.

O red pomegranate of thy perfect mouth!
    My lips' life-fruitage, might I taste and die,
Here in thy garden, where the scented south
    Wind chastens agony;

Reap death from thy live lips in one long kiss,
    And look my last into thine eyes and rest:
What sweets had life to me sweeter than this
      Swift dying on thy breast?

Or, if that may not be, for Love's sake, Dear!
    Keep silence still, and dream that we shall lie,
Red mouth to mouth, entwined, and always hear
      The south wind's melody,

Here in thy garden, through the sighing boughs,
    Beyond the reach of time and chance and change,
And bitter life and death, and broken vows,
      That sadden and estrange.

SERAPHITA.

Come not before me now, O visionary face!
Me tempest-tost, and borne along life's passionate sea;
Troublous and dark and stormy though my passage be;
Not here and now may we commingle or embrace,
Lest the loud anguish of the waters should efface
The bright illumination of thy memory,
Which dominates the night: rest, far away from me,
In the serenity of thine abiding-place!

But when the storm is highest, and the thunders blare,
And sea and sky are riven, O moon of all my night!
Stoop down but once in pity of my great despair,
And let thine hand, though over late to help, alight
But once upon my pale eyes and my drowning hair,
Before the great waves conquer in the last vain fight.

EPIGRAM.

Because I am idolatrous and have besought,
With grievous supplication and consuming prayer,
The admirable image that my dreams have wrought
Out of her swan's neck and her dark, abundant hair:
The jealous gods, who brook no worship save their own,
Turned my live idol marble and her heart to stone.

QUID NON SPEREMUS, AMANTES?

For ARTHUR MOORE.

Why is there in the least touch of her hands
    More grace than other women's lips bestow,
If love is but a slave in fleshly bands
    Of flesh to flesh, wherever love may go?

Why choose vain grief and heavy-hearted hours
    For her lost voice, and dear remembered hair,
If love may cull his honey from all flowers,
    And girls grow thick as violets, everywhere?

Nay! She is gone, and all things fall apart;
    Or she is cold, and vainly have we prayed;
And broken is the summer's splendid heart,
    And hope within a deep, dark grave is laid.

As man aspires and falls, yet a soul springs
    Out of his agony of flesh at last,
So love that flesh enthralls, shall rise on wings
    Soul-centred, when the rule of flesh is past.

Then, most High Love, or wreathed with myrtle sprays,
    Or crownless and forlorn, nor less a star,
Thee may I serve and follow, all my days,
    Whose thorns are sweet as never roses are!

CHANSON SANS PAROLES.

In the deep violet air,
   Not a leaf is stirred;
   There is no sound heard,
But afar, the rare
   Trilled voice of a bird.

Is the wood's dim heart,
   And the fragrant pine,
   Incense, and a shrine
Of her coming? Apart,
   I wait for a sign.

What the sudden hush said,
   She will hear, and forsake,
   Swift, for my sake,
Her green, grassy bed:
   She will hear and awake!

She will hearken and glide,
   From her place of deep rest,
   Dove-eyed, with the breast
Of a dove, to my side:
   The pines bow their crest.

I wait for a sign:
>The leaves to be waved,
>The tall tree-tops laved
In a flood of sunshine,
>This world to be saved!

In the deep violet air,
>*Not a leaf is stirred;*
>*There is no sound heard,*
But afar, the rare
>*Trilled voice of a bird.*

THE PIERROT OF THE MINUTE

A DRAMATIC PHANTASY IN ONE ACT

THE CHARACTERS

A Moon Maiden

Pierrot

THE SCENE

A glade in the Parc du Petit Trianon.
In the centre a Doric temple with steps coming down the stage.
On the left a little Cupid on a pedestal.
Twilight.

(Pierrot enters with his hands full of lilies. He is burdened with a little basket. He stands gazing at the Temple and the Statue.)

PIERROT.

My journey's end! This surely is the glade
Which I was promised: I have well obeyed!
A clue of lilies was I bid to find,
Where the green alleys most obscurely wind;
Where tall oaks darkliest canopy o'erhead,
And moss and violet make the softest bed;
Where the path ends, and leagues behind me lie
The gleaming courts and gardens of Versailles;
The lilies streamed before me, green and white;
I gathered, following: they led me right,   10
To the bright temple and the sacred grove:
This is, in truth, the very shrine of Love!

(He gathers together his flowers and lays them at the foot of Cupid's statue; then he goes timidly up the first steps of the temple and stops.)

It is so solitary, I grow afraid.
Is there no priest here, no devoted maid?
Is there no oracle, no voice to speak,
Interpreting to me the word I seek?

(A very gentle music of lutes floats out from the temple. Pierrot starts back; he shows extreme surprise; then he returns to the foreground, and crouches down in rapt attention until the music ceases. His face grows puzzled and petulant.)

> Too soon! too soon! in that enchanting strain,
> Days yet unlived, I almost lived again:
> It almost taught me that I most would know —
> Why am I here, and why am I Pierrot?   20

(Absently he picks up a lily which has fallen to the ground, and repeats:)

> Why came I here, and why am I Pierrot?
> That music and this silence both affright;
> Pierrot can never be a friend of night.
> I never felt my solitude before —
> Once safe at home, I will return no more.
> Yet the commandment of the scroll was plain;
> While the light lingers let me read again.

(He takes a scroll from his bosom and reads:)

> *'He loves to-night who never loved before;*
> *Who ever loved, to-night shall love once more.'*
> I never loved! I know not what love is.   30
> I am so ignorant — but what is this?

(Reads)

> *'Who would adventure to encounter Love*
> *Must rest one night within this hallowed grove.*
> *Cast down thy lilies, which have led thee on,*
> *Before the tender feet of Cupidon.'*
> Thus much is done, the night remains to me.
> Well, Cupidon, be my security!
> Here is more writing, but too faint to read.

(He puzzles for a moment, then casts the scroll down.)

> Hence, vain old parchment. I have learnt thy rede!

(He looks round uneasily, starts at his shadow; then discovers his basket with glee. He takes out a flask of wine, pours it into a glass, and drinks.)

> *Courage, mon Ami!* I shall never miss   40
> Society with such a friend as this.
> How merrily the rosy bubbles pass,
> Across the amber crystal of the glass.
> I had forgotten you. Methinks this quest
> Can wake no sweeter echo in my breast.

(Looks round at the statue, and starts.)

> Nay, little god! forgive. I did but jest.

(He fills another glass, and pours it upon the statue.)

> This libation, Cupid, take,
>   With the lilies at thy feet;
> Cherish Pierrot for their sake
>   Send him visions strange and sweet,   50
> While he slumbers at thy feet.
> Only love kiss him awake!
>   *Only love kiss him awake!*

(Slowly falls the darkness, soft music plays, while Pierrot gathers together fern and foliage into a rough couch at the foot of the steps which lead to the Temple d'Amour. Then he lies down upon it, having made his prayer. It is night.)

(Softly.)   Music, more music, far away and faint:
> It is an echo of mine heart's complaint.
> Why should I be so musical and sad?
> I wonder why I used to be so glad?

In single glee I chased blue butterflies,
Half butterfly myself, but not so wise,
For they were twain, and I was only one.   60
Ah me! how pitiful to be alone.
My brown birds told me much, but in mine ear
They never whispered this — I learned it here:
The soft wood sounds, the rustlings in the breeze,
Are but the stealthy kisses of the trees.
Each flower and fern in this enchanted wood
Leans to her fellow, and is understood;
The eglantine, in loftier station set,
Stoops down to woo the maidly violet.
In gracile pairs the very lilies grow: 70
None is companionless except Pierrot.
Music, more music! how its echoes steal
Upon my senses with unlooked for weal.
Tired am I, tired, and far from this lone glade
Seems mine old joy in rout and masquerade.
Sleep cometh over me, now will I prove,
By Cupid's grace, what is this thing called love.

(Sleeps.)

(There is more music of lutes for an interval, during which a bright radiance, white and cold, streams from the temple upon the face of Pierrot. Presently a Moon Maiden steps out of the temple; she descends and stands over the sleeper.)

THE LADY.

Who is this mortal
    Who ventures to-night
To woo an immortal,   80
    Cold, cold the moon's light,

126

For sleep at this portal,
Bold lover of night.
Fair is the mortal
In soft, silken white,
Who seeks an immortal.
Ah, lover of night,
Be warned at the portal,
And save thee in flight!

(She stoops over him: Pierrot stirs in his sleep.)

PIERROT *(Murmuring).*

Forget not, Cupid. Teach me all thy lore: 90
'He loves to-night who never loved before.'

THE LADY.

Unwitting boy! when, be it soon or late,
What Pierrot ever has escaped his fate?
What if I warned him! He might yet evade,
Through the long windings of this verdant glade;
Seek his companions in the blither way,
Which, else, must be as lost as yesterday.
So might he still pass some unheeding hours
In the sweet company of birds and flowers.
How fair he is, with red lips formed for joy,   100
As softly curved as those of Venus' boy.
Methinks his eyes, beneath their silver sheaves,
Rest tranquilly like lilies under leaves.
Arrayed in innocence, what touch of grace
Reveals the scion of a courtly race?
Well, I will warn him, though, I fear, too late —
What Pierrot ever has escaped his fate?
But, see, he stirs, new knowledge fires his brain,

127

And Cupid's vision bids him wake again.
Dione's Daughter! but how fair he is,   110
Would it be wrong to rouse him with a kiss?

(She stoops down and kisses him, then withdraws into the shadow.)

PIERROT *(Rubbing his eyes)*.

Celestial messenger! remain, remain;
Or, if a vision, visit me again!
What is this light, and whither am I come
To sleep beneath the stars so far from home?

(Rises slowly to his feet.)

PIERROT.

Stay, I remember this is Venus' Grove,
And I am hither come to encounter —

THE LADY*(Coming forward, but veiled)*.

Love!

PIERROT *(In ecstasy, throwing himself at her feet)*.

Then have I ventured and encountered Love?

THE LADY.

Not yet, rash boy! and, if thou wouldst be wise,
Return unknowing; he is safe who flies.   120

PIERROT.

Never, sweet lady, will I leave this place
Until I see the wonder of thy face.
Goddess or Naiad! lady of this Grove,
Made mortal for a night to teach me love,
Unveil thyself, although thy beauty be
Too luminous for my mortality.

THE LADY*(Unveiling)*.

Then, foolish boy, receive at length thy will:
Now knowest thou the greatness of thine ill.

PIERROT.

Now have I lost my heart, and gained my goal.

THE LADY.

Didst thou not read the warning on the scroll?   130

PIERROT*(Picking up the parchment)*.

I read it all, as on this quest I fared,
Save where it was illegible and hard.

THE LADY.

Alack! poor scholar, wast thou never taught
A little knowledge serveth less than naught?
Hadst thou perused — but, stay, I will explain
What was the writing which thou didst disdain.

(Reads)

'*Au Petit Trianon*, at night's full noon,
Mortal, beware the kisses of the moon!
Whoso seeks her she gathers like a flower —
He gives a life, and only gains an hour.'   140

PIERROT *(Laughing recklessly)*.

Bear me away to thine enchanted bower,
All of my life I venture for an hour.

THE LADY.

Take up thy destiny of short delight;
I am thy lady for a summer's night.
Lift up your viols, maidens of my train,

And work such havoc on this mortal's brain
That for a moment he may touch and know
Immortal things, and be full Pierrot.
White music, Nymphs! Violet and Eglantine!
To stir his tired veins like magic wine.   150
What visitants across his spirit glance,
Lying on lilies, while he watch me dance?
Watch, and forget all weary things of earth,
All memories and cares, all joy and mirth,
While my dance wooes him, light and rythmical,
And weaves his heart into my coronal.
Music, more music for his soul's delight:
Love is his lady for a summer's night.

(Pierrot reclines, and gazes at her while she dances. The dance finished, she beckons to him: he rises dreamily, and stands at her side.)

PIERROT.

Whence came, dear Queen, such magic melody?

THE LADY.

Pan made it long ago in Arcady.   160

PIERROT.

I heard it long ago, I know not where,
As I knew thee, or ever I came here.
But I forget all things — my name and race,
All that I ever knew except thy face.
Who art thou, lady? Breathe a name to me,
That I may tell it like a rosary.
Thou, whom I sought, dear Dryad of the trees,
How art thou designate — art thou Heart's-Ease?

THE LADY.

Waste not the night in idle questioning,
Since Love departs at dawn's awakening.   170

PIERROT.

Nay, thou art right; what recks thy name or state,
Since thou art lovely and compassionate.
Play out thy will on me: I am thy lyre.

THE LADY.

I am to each the face of his desire.

PIERROT.

I am not Pierrot, but Venus' dove,
Who craves a refuge on the breast of love.

THE LADY.

What wouldst thou of the maiden of the moon?
Until the cock crow I may grant thy boon.

PIERROT.

Then, sweet Moon Maiden, in some magic car,
Wrought wondrously of many a homeless star —   180
Such must attend thy journeys through the skies, —
Drawn by a team of milk-white butterflies,
Whom, with soft voice and music of thy maids,
Thou urgest gently through the heavenly glades;
Mount me beside thee, bear me far away
From the low regions of the solar day;
Over the rainbow, up into the moon,
Where is thy palace and thine opal throne;
There on thy bosom —

THE LADY.

Too ambitious boy!
I did but promise thee one hour of joy.   190
This tour thou plannest, with a heart so light,
Could hardly be completed in a night.
Hast thou no craving less remote than this?

PIERROT.

Would it be impudent to beg a kiss?

THE LADY.

I say not that: yet prithee have a care!
Often audacity has proved a snare.
How wan and pale do moon-kissed roses grow —
Dost thou not fear my kisses, Pierrot?

PIERROT.

As one who faints upon the Libyan plain
Fears the oasis which brings life again!   200

THE LADY.

Where far away green palm trees seem to stand
May be a mirage of the wreathing sand.

PIERROT.

Nay, dear enchantress, I consider naught,
Save mine own ignorance, which would be taught.

THE LADY.

Dost thou persist?

PIERROT.

I do entreat this boon!
(She bends forward, their lips meet: she withdraws with a petulant shiver. She utters a peal of clear laughter.)

THE LADY.

Why art thou pale, fond lover of the moon?

PIERROT.

Cold are thy lips, more cold than I can tell;
Yet would I hang on them, thine icicle!
Cold is thy kiss, more cold than I could dream
Arcturus sits, watching the Boreal stream: 210
But with its frost such sweetness did conspire
That all my veins are filled with running fire;
Never I knew that life contained such bliss
As the divine completeness of a kiss.

THE LADY.

Apt scholar! so love's lesson has been taught,
Warning, as usual, has gone for naught.

PIERROT.

Had all my schooling been of this soft kind,
To play the truant I were less inclined.
Teach me again! I am a sorry dunce —
I never knew a task by conning once.   220

THE LADY.

Then come with me! below this pleasant shrine
Of Venus we will presently recline,
Until birds' twitter beckon me away
To mine own home, beyond the milky-way.
I will instruct thee, for I deem as yet
Of Love thou knowest but the alphabet.

PIERROT.

In its sweet grammar I shall grow most wise,
If all its rules be written in thine eyes.

(The lady sits upon a step of the temple, and Pierrot leans upon his elbow at her feet, regarding her.)

PIERROT.

Sweet contemplation! how my senses yearn
To be thy scholar always, always learn.   230
Hold not so high from me thy radiant mouth,
Fragrant with all the spices of the South;
Nor turn, O sweet! thy golden face away,
For with it goes the light of all my day.
Let me peruse it, till I know by rote
Each line of it, like music, note by note;
Raise thy long lashes, Lady! smile again:
These studies profit me.

(Taking her hand.)

THE LADY.

Refrain, refrain!

PIERROT (*With passion*).

I am but studious, so do not stir;
Thou art my star, I thine astronomer!   240
Geometry was founded on thy lip.

(Kisses her hand.)

THE LADY.

This attitude becomes not scholarship!
Thy zeal I praise; but, prithee, not so fast,
Nor leave the rudiments until the last.
Science applied is good, but t'were a schism
To study such before the catechism.
Bear thee more modestly, while I submit
Some easy problems to confirm thy wit.

PIERROT.

In all humility my mind I pit
Against her problems which would test my wit.   250

THE LADY *(Questioning him from a little book bound deliciously in vellum).*

What is Love?
Is it a folly,
Is it mirth, or melancholy?
Joys above,
Are there many, or not any?
What is love?

PIERROT *(Answering in a very humble attitude of scholarship).*

If you please,
A most sweet folly!
Full of mirth and melancholy:
Both of these!   260
In its sadness worth all gladness,
If you please!

THE LADY.

Prithee where,
Goes Love a-hiding?
Is he long in his abiding
Anywhere?
Can you bind him when you find him;
Prithee, where?

PIERROT.

With spring days
Love comes and dallies: 270
Upon the mountains, through the valleys
Lie Love's ways.

Then he leaves you and deceives you
  In spring days.

THE LADY.

Thine answers please me: 'tis thy turn to ask.
To meet thy questioning be now my task.

PIERROT.

Since I know thee, dear Immortal,
Is my heart become a blossom,
To be worn upon thy bosom.
When thou turn me from this portal,   280
Whither shall I, hapless mortal,
Seek love out and win again
Heart of me that thou retain?

THE LADY.

In and out the woods and valleys,
Circling, soaring like a swallow,
Love shall flee and thou shalt follow:
Though he stops awhile and dallies,
Never shalt thou stay his malice!
Moon-kissed mortals seek in vain
To possess their hearts again!   290

PIERROT.

Tell me, Lady, shall I never
Rid me of this grievous burden!
Follow Love and find his guerdon
In no maiden whatsoever?
Wilt thou hold my heart for ever?
Rather would I thine forget,
In some earthly Pierrette!

THE LADY.

Thus thy fate, whate'er thy will is!
Moon-struck child, go seek my traces
Vainly in all mortal faces!   300
In and out among the lilies,
Court each rural Amaryllis:
Seek the signet of Love's hand
In each courtly Corisande!

PIERROT.

Now, verily, sweet maid, of school I tire:
These answers are not such as I desire.

THE LADY.

Why art thou sad?

PIERROT.

         I dare not tell.

THE LADY *(Caressingly)*.

              Come, say!

PIERROT.

Is love all schooling, with no time to play?

THE LADY.

Though all love's lessons be a holiday,
Yet I will humour thee: what wouldst thou play?   310

PIERROT.

What are the games that small moon-maids enjoy,
Or is their time all spent in staid employ?

THE LADY.

Sedate they are, yet games they much enjoy:
They skip with stars, the rainbow is their toy.

PIERROT.

That is too hard!

THE LADY.

For mortal's play.

PIERROT.

What then?

THE LADY.

Teach me some pastime from the world of men.

PIERROT.

I have it, maiden.

THE LADY.

Can it soon be taught?

PIERROT.

A simple game, I learnt it at the Court.
I sit by thee.

THE LADY.

But, prithee, not so near.

PIERROT.

That is essential, as will soon appear.   320
Lay here thine hand, which cold night dews anoint,
Washing its white —

THE LADY.

Now is this to the point?

PIERROT.

Prithee, forbear! Such is the game's design.

THE LADY.

Here is my hand.

PIERROT.

I cover it with mine.

THE LADY.

What must I next?

(They play.)

PIERROT.

Withdraw.

THE LADY.

It goes too fast.

(They continue playing, until Pierrot catches her hand.)

PIERROT *(Laughing).*

Tis done. I win my forfeit at the last.

(He tries to embrace her. She escapes; he chases her round the stage; she eludes him.)

THE LADY.

Thou art not quick enough. Who hopes to catch
A moon-beam, must use twice as much despatch.

PIERROT *(Sitting down sulkily).*

I grow aweary, and my heart is sore.
Thou dost not love me; I will play no more.   330

(He buries his face in his hands: the lady stands over him.)

THE LADY.

What is this petulance?

139

PIERROT.

'Tis quick to tell —
Thou hast but mocked me.

THE LADY.

Nay! I love thee well!

PIERROT.

Repeat those words, for still within my breast
A whisper warns me they are said in jest.

THE LADY.

I jested not: at daybreak I must go,
Yet loving thee far better than thou know.

PIERROT.

Then, by this altar, and this sacred shrine,
Take my sworn troth, and swear thee wholly mine!
The gods have wedded mortals long ere this.

THE LADY.

There was enough betrothal in my kiss.   340
What need of further oaths?

PIERROT.

That bound not thee!

THE LADY.

Peace! since I tell thee that it may not be.
But sit beside me whilst I soothe thy bale
With some moon fancy or celestial tale.

PIERROT.

Tell me of thee, and that dim, happy place
Where lies thine home, with maidens of thy race!

THE LADY (*Seating herself*).

Calm is it yonder, very calm; the air
For mortals' breath is too refined and rare;
Hard by a green lagoon our palace rears
Its dome of agate through a myriad years.   350
A hundred chambers its bright walls enthrone,
Each one carved strangely from a precious stone.
Within the fairest, clad in purity,
Our mother dwelleth immemorially:
Moon-calm, moon-pale, with moon stones on her gown
The floor she treads with little pearls is sown;
She sits upon a throne of amethysts,
And orders mortal fortunes as she lists;
I, and my sisters, all around her stand,
And, when she speaks, accomplish her demand.   360

PIERROT.

Methought grim Clotho and her sisters twain
With shrivelled fingers spun this web of bane!

THE LADY.

Theirs and my mother's realm is far apart;
Hers is the lustrous kingdom of the heart,
And dreamers all, and all who sing and love,
Her power acknowledge, and her rule approve.

PIERROT.

Me, even me, she hath led into this grove.

THE LADY.

Yea, thou art one of hers! But, ere this night,
Often I watched my sisters take their flight
Down heaven's stairway of the clustered stars   370

To gaze on mortals through their lattice bars;
And some in sleep they woo with dreams of bliss
Too shadowy to tell, and some they kiss.
But all to whom they come, my sisters say,
Forthwith forget all joyance of the day,
Forget their laughter and forget their tears,
And dream away with singing all their years —
Moon-lovers always!

(She sighs.)

PIERROT.

Why art sad, sweet Moon?

(Laughing.)

THE LADY.

For this, my story, grant me now a boon.

PIERROT.

I am thy servitor.

THE LADY.

Would, then, I knew   380
More of the earth, what men and women do.

PIERROT.

I will explain.

THE LADY.

Let brevity attend
Thy wit, for night approaches to its end.

PIERROT.

Once was I a page at Court, so trust in me:
That's the first lesson of society.

142

THE LADY.

Society?

PIERROT.

I mean the very best
Pardy! thou wouldst not hear about the rest.
I know it not, but am a *petit maître*
At rout and festival and *bal champêtre*.
But since example be instruction's ease,   390
Let's play the thing. — Now, Madame, if you please!

(He helps her to rise, and leads her forward: then he kisses her hand, bowing over it with a very courtly air.)

THE LADY.

What am I, then?

PIERROT.

A most divine Marquise!
Perhaps that attitude hath too much ease.

(Passes her.)

Ah, that is better! To complete the plan,
Nothing is necessary save a fan.

THE LADY.

Cool is the night, what needs it?

PIERROT.

Madame, pray
Reflect, it is essential to our play.

THE LADY *(Taking a lily).*

Here is my fan!

PIERROT.

So, use it with intent:
The deadliest arm in beauty's armament!

THE LADY.

What do we next?

PIERROT.

We talk!

THE LADY.

But what about?   400

PIERROT.

We quiz the company and praise the rout;
Are polished, petulant, malicious, sly,
Or what you will, so reputations die.
Observe the Duchess in Venetian lace,
With the red eminence.

THE LADY.

A pretty face!

PIERROT.

For something tarter set thy wits to search —
'She loves the churchman better than the church.'

THE LADY.

Her blush is charming; would it were her own!

PIERROT.

Madame is merciless!

THE LADY.

Is that the tone?

PIERROT.

The very tone: I swear thou lackest naught,   410
Madame was evidently bred at Court.

THE LADY.

Thou speakest glibly: 'tis not of thine age.

PIERROT.

I listened much, as best becomes a page.

THE LADY.

I like thy Court but little —

PIERROT.

            Hush! the Queen!
Bow, but not low — thou knowest what I mean.

THE LADY.

Nay, that I know not!

PIERROT.

        Though she wear a crown,
'Tis from La Pompadour one fears a frown.

THE LADY.

Thou art a child: thy malice is a game.

PIERROT.

A most sweet pastime — scandal is its name.

THE LADY.

Enough, it wearies me.

PIERROT.

        Then, rare Marquise,   420
Desert the crowd to wander through the trees.

(He bows low, and she curtsies; they move round the stage. When they pass before the Statue he seizes her hand and falls on his knee.)

THE LADY.

What wouldst thou now?

PIERROT.

            Ah, prithee, what, save thee!

THE LADY.

Was this included in thy comedy?

PIERROT.

Ah, mock me not! In vain with quirk and jest
I strive to quench the passion in my breast;
In vain thy blandishments would make me play:
Still I desire far more than I can say.
My knowledge halts, ah, sweet, be piteous,
Instruct me still, while time remains to us,
Be what thou wist, Goddess, moon-maid, *Marquise,*   430
So that I gather from thy lips heart's ease,
Nay, I implore thee, think thee how time flies!

THE LADY.

Hush! I beseech thee, even now night dies.

PIERROT.

Night, day, are one to me for thy soft sake.

(He entreats her with imploring gestures, she hesitates: then puts her finger on her lip, hushing him.)

THE LADY.

It is too late, for hark! the birds awake.

PIERROT.

The birds awake! It is the voice of day!

THE LADY.

Farewell, dear youth! They summon me away.

(The light changes, it grows daylight: and music imitates the twitter of the birds. They stand gazing at the morning: then Pierrot sinks back upon his bed, he covers his face in his hands.)

THE LADY

(Bending over him).

> Music, my maids! His weary senses steep
> In soft untroubled and oblivious sleep,
> With mandragore anoint his tirèd eyes,   440
> That they may open on mere memories,
> Then shall a vision seem his lost delight,
> With love, his lady for a summer's night.
> Dream thou hast dreamt all this, when thou awake,
> Yet still be sorrowful, for a dream's sake.
> I leave thee, sleeper! Yea, I leave thee now,
> Yet take my legacy upon thy brow:
> Remember me, who was compassionate,
> And opened for thee once, the ivory gate.
> I come no more, thou shalt not see my face   450
> When I am gone to mine exalted place:
> Yet all thy days are mine, dreamer of dreams,
> All silvered over with the moon's pale beams:
> Go forth and seek in each fair face in vain,
> To find the image of thy love again.
> All maids are kind to thee, yet never one

147

Shall hold thy truant heart till day be done.
Whom once the moon has kissed, loves long and late,
Yet never finds the maid to be his mate.
Farewell, dear sleeper, follow out thy fate.   460

(The Moon Maiden withdraws: a song is sung from behind: it is full day.)

THE MOON MAIDEN'S SONG

Sleep! Cast thy canopy
    Over this sleeper's brain,
Dim grow his memory,
    When he awake again.

Love stays a summer night,
    Till lights of morning come;
Then takes her wingèd flight
    Back to her starry home.

Sleep! Yet thy days are mine;
    Love's seal is over thee: 470
Far though my ways from thine,
    Dim though thy memory.

Love stays a summer night,
    Till lights of morning come;
Then takes her wingèd flight
    Back to her starry home.

(When the song is finished, the curtain falls upon Pierrot sleeping.)

THE END

TRANSLATIONS FROM *LA PUCELLE*

LA PUCELLE

VARIANT OF CANTO XVII[1]
CORISANDRE

My reader by experience is acquaint
That the fair god, whom as a child they paint,
(Though childish games are hardly all his sport)
Hath quivers two, of very different sort.
The one holds arrows, whose entrancing sting
Is felt with little risk or suffering;
These grow with time, and penetrate the heart,
Leaving the lively wounds they there impart.
Like raging fire, his other arrows fly,
Swift from the bow and burning instantly,   10
On senses five destruction fell they wreak,
With lively red illuminate the cheek;
With a new blood, men feel their bodies fired,
And with new being, hold themselves inspired.
Nothing they understand, their eyes are bright,
Gesture and action follow their mad flight.
Waters which boil tumultuous on the fire,
Which, o'er the copper's brink, rise and retire,
Which run away and leap and fall and waltz,
Are but an image, incomplete and false,   20
Of love's fierce fire, when once it agitates:
You know it, brethren mine, and all its states!

---

[1] This Canto, being completely different in the other editions is translated here in its entirety as a variant. It was the fourteenth Canto in the editions in eighteen Cantos and the nineteenth in those of twenty-four. [*Note from original edition.*]

151

But this capricious god, our light love's king,
Contrived anon a far more pleasant thing:
Betwixt Cutendre and Blois, he caused to dwell
A beauteous maid, whose aspect amiable
Had left the charms of Agnes far behind,
If, with her beauty, her heart had been kind.
(A kind heart's worth much beauty in a dame!)
Foolish and young, Corisandre was her name.   30
Love's will it was, each king or cavalier,
Young bachelor or magistrate severe,
Should seek, grown foolish, being overfond
With this fair idiot a closer bond;
Servants, the people and the viler herd
Alone exempt were from this law absurd;
Gentle or kingly race one had to own
Thus to grow mad. Nor was it that alone:
The healing art, as much hemp as you will,
Brought little help and succour 'gainst this ill;   40
And worse and worse the brain would daily grow,
Till the fair fool would some complaisance show,
And such a time in destiny was writ
That, at the last, she might attain to wit.

On Loire's banks nurtured, lovers, more than one,
For Corisandre's sight, were all undone;
One, losing memory and sense, for food
Just as a stag, would pasture in the wood;
And one would think his buttocks were of glass,
And being jostled by the folk who pass,   50
Would weep because his back-side had been broke.
Goyon is sure he is of female folk,
Wears petticoats and dies of his despairs,
Because, to truss them up no lover cares:
A saddle *Valori* takes, by no means light;
He thinks himself an ass — is doubtless right —
Asks for his load, and ceases not to bray.
Sablé, transformed into a saucepot's way,
On three feet walks; upon the ground, one hand,
And one bow-legged. Alas, in this our land,   60

Amongst the madmen we might well have been,
Though the fair Corisandre we ne'er had seen.
Who is the sapient wit, who has not once,
Through his desires, been proved a very dunce?
Who has not had a check? In prose or verse,
All men are madmen, if they are not worse.

   Now Corisandre a grandmother possessed,
Though stiff, a worthy dame by all confessed,
Whose pride, though she concealed it in the shade,
Was to behold the fools her daughter made.   70
But scruples 'gan her mind at last to urge,
Sorry she was for such a dismal scourge.
Her daughter then so fatal to the mind,
Within an hidden chamber she confined.
Before the castle she took care to place
Custodians two, with a forbidding face,
Ready the house's entrance to maintain
Against all comers, who would risk their brain.
The foolish Fair, to such seclusion brought,
Sang, sewed, embroidered, very little thought,   80
Regret or care, not e'en the least desire
Moved her to heal her lovers' maddened fire,
Though had the beauty had this tenderness,
All it had cost her, would be to say Yes.

   The haughty Chandos, in high anger still
That his proud combatant had 'scaped his skill,
Straight to his Britons in his wrath returns;
E'en as the hound, whose savage jaw which yearns
Has snapped in vain at the escaping hare,
Tums, while his yelps of anger rend the air,   90
Then to his master with slow steps will go,
Head hanging down, and long tail drooping low.
Well his unworthy animal he cursed
Who, in soft duel, brought him off the worst.
His general withal, hastes to supply
A youthful colonel, happening to be by;
Bold Irishman, by name Paul Tirconel,

Whose chest was broad, who bore himself right well,
As stout of arm as limb, with iron spine,
Whose haughty brow was sealed with the consign   100
Of one who never such affronts would face,
As now made Chandos redden in disgrace.

This martial pair, with gallant throng behind,
The gates of Corisandre's house now find;
They seek to enter, when the porters cry:
"We bid you halt; bethink you ere you try
To enter here and Corisandre behold,
If you would wish what wits you have to hold."
Proud Chandos this a further insult deems,
Onward he rushes, while his fury teems;   110
With one straight blow, he sends twelve yards away
One porter, with his arm put out of play;
Aching and bruised he lies upon the sand.
Paul Tirconel, with no less ruthless hand,
Spurs on his fiery steed and whips him twice,
Presses his knees, lets rein and in a trice
The courser like a lightning flash has sped
And passes o'er the other porter's head;
Lifting his front, a moment still he gazed,
A moment rests astonished and amazed,   120
Then turning round receives a doughty blow,
Which, like his erstwhile colleague, lays him low.
So in the province, some gay officer,
A dandy, natty, fond of sport and stir,
Runs to the play amain, the porter beats
And, without paying, from his ravished seats
He hisses everything he contemplates.

The English suite within the courtyard swarm;
The ancient Dame descends in high alarm,
While Corisandre, affrighted at the noise,   130
Her kirtle dons and from her room deploys.
Chandos addresses her a salute short,
True Englishman! much speech was not his forte;
But when he saw a face so innocent,

That lily-skin, those charms so succulent,
Those budding breasts and arms of ivory,
Which nature's hands had rounded artfully,
A happy chance he vowed was his to seize;
When Corisandre, with mien not quite at ease,
Casts him a glance which little seemed to say.   140
For Paul Tirconel, in his courteous way,
Saluted both the daughter and the dame,
And ogled in his turn and felt love's flame.
What happened then? Alas, fell madness came.

Chandos, affected by that malady,
As horse-dealer, native of Normandy,
The youthful fair declares to be a horse,
Who must be saddled, mounted in due course,
He whips her fleshy saddle with a crack,
And in a trice is mounted on her back.   150
The fair cries out, and under Chandos falls.
Paul Tirconel, whom different mania calls,
A tavern-keeper holds himself to be,
And takes the fair, who's crouched upon her knee,
For a fat tun of wine, which he must bore,
Good wine and lees from th'orifice to draw.
Still straddling her, Chandos cries out: "Have done,
God dam! You're mad, I think; the evil one
Has crossed your wits; you cannot even tell
From tun of wine, my white mare Isabel!..."   160
"It is my tun, my tap's occasion."
"It is my horse..." "My brother, 't is my tun..."
Both were exactly certain they were right,
And for their mad opinion fain to fight,
With just such fire, as monks in angry vein,
Devotion of their scapular maintain,
Or d'Olivet upholds his Cicero.
Swift contradictions rattle to and fro,
And certain words, which, thank my modesty,
I spare my readers' ears; vocabulary   170
Which, loathed by proper pride, our Britons famed,
Who vaunt their sabres, look on unashamed.

As winds, which gather force, though erstwhile weak,
Are roused and growl and fragile vessels break,
Which toss too much the waters to withstand,
Horror is shed by them o'er all the land —
So our two Englishmen at first were viewed
In laughter's semblance and a joking mood;
Then vexed, delirious fancies on them steal,
They both rush on, determined death to deal.   180
Both are on guard, in a like posture shown,
With outstretched arms and bodies forward thrown,
In quart, in tierce, their tough skins they attack.
But soon all rule and measure 'gin to lack,
As hotter still, and fiercer, more incensed
With slashing blows of the keen steel they fenced.
Less fierce in Etna's forge the one-eyed crew,
Out of the anvil, fiery sparks pursue,
Beneath less heavy hammers, who prepare
For thunder's master his big cannon there.   190

On every side blood casts a lavish stain,
From neck and arm and from the riven brain,
But not one cry succeeded to the wound;
The worthy dame would cure them *sans* a sound,
To strip them of their armour she desired,
A *Pater* said, a confessor required:
Her daughter all the time, with languid view,
Bridled and sought her coiffure to renew.
Our British pair, exhausted, drenched in gore,
Were lying both full length upon the floor,   200
When who should come but the great King of France
With all his gallant knights, who bore the lance,
And those bright fair, within his court, who throve
Worthy of Mars and of the God of Love.
Beholding these, the beauteous Fool draws nigh,
And humbly drops a clumsy curtesy,
Bids them good day with utter nonchalance,
And looks at all things with indifference.
Who e'er had thought that nature would admit
Poison so much in eyes so lacking wit.   210

The beauty even hardly deigns to glance
At the distracted, handsome heads of France.
Heaven sheds its benign graces every day,
Which mortals take in very different way;
All things are fashioned to the time and place,
And very diverse are the effects of grace.
The self-same sap when nourished in the earth,
Of divers fruits the essences of birth,
Produces pinks, the thistle and the rose;
And d'Argens sighs when d'Arget laughter knows.   220
Maupertuis of folly's as prolific
As Newton of his theories scientific.
A certain king to use his soldiers knows
As often for his loves as 'gainst his foes.
All's variable; and in a different strain
Function the British and the Gallic brain:
Each one the customs of his country fits;
With Englishmen, of hard and sombre wits,
Madness is atrabilious, black as night;
But with the French, it lively is and light.   230

Our folk the hands of one and other seize,
Dance in a ring, sing choruses that please.
The fat Bonneau exertions makes immense,
Though just as scant of breath as of cadence;
While Father Bonifoux, psalter in hand,
Dances with slower steps with the mad band;
Him doth the page, above the rest, beguile,
Though by his pious language and his smile,
His accent, gestures and his eyes so kind,
It seemed the Father had a rag of mind.   240

That novel ill which fascinates the view
Of this most royal and fantastic crew,
Leads them the castle's great court-yard to deem
A garden, wherein flows a pleasant stream.
They wish to bathe, their clothes and corslets pass,
And nakedly disport them on the grass,
Swim in the void, and lift aloft the chin,

Thinking clear water covers them within.
The monk, the while he swam, 't is meet to note,
From the enchanting page was ne'er remote.   250

At such a mass of noddles without brain,
Such nudity, our modest fair with pain,
The Maid and Agnes and fair Dorothy
Discreetly turned their head and shut the eye,
Then looked again, then after once again
Eyes, heart and hand to the celestial plain.
"Have I then come," cried Joan, "to such a pass?
I have St. Denis for me and mine ass;
And many an impious Briton I have braved,
Avenged my prince, and many a convent saved;   260
T'wards Orléans' walls my stressful way I've ta'en;
And Destiny must make my labour vain —
Our heroes mad?" Agnes and Dorothy
Contained themselves with certain difficulty;
Sometimes they laughed, sometimes were passing sad
To see great kings and noble heroes mad.
But what to do? Where fly? Oh, whither get?
Cutendre's castle they might well regret;
Had not a servant, of her secret lore,
Taught them the art wits wandering to restore.   270
"Good sense once lost," she said, "'t is Fate's decree,
To brains whence it has flown, restored can be,
Only when Corisandre the fair will deign
In snares of love to let herself be ta'en"

This good advice was not without avail,
The muleteer to heed it did not fail:
Doubtless you know that lecher of remark
Was always amorous of Joan of Arc,
And jealous of the ass, discreet of walk,
That Amazon he never ceased to stalk.   280
When thus he heard, in confidence arrayed,
He starts forthwith his King and France to aid.
Just in a corner chanced the fair to lie,
Whom from afar he had been pleased to spy;

T'wards her he runs, well armed with fire and rage.
They thought him mad, who was the only sage.
O muleteer! on thee what treasures rare
Kind nature had bestowed with partial care,
Thy lowly fortune compensating well.
With one swift bound he subjugates the belle.   290
He lays her low and with a vigorous thrust,
A very ram he plays the game of lust,
He forces, breaks the four-fold barricade;
Then quickening the action of his blade
In all its length, he lodges for reward,
Within its sheath his most victorious sword.
At such a brisk assault the youthful fair,
For self-defence had scanty time to spare;
But with clenched fists, with all her body prone,
Biting her lips, her straight limbs backward thrown,   300
Nothing by her was understood or known:
She only waited and invoked her saint,
Until her adversary's loins grew faint.

    To her, in fine, the pleasing moment came
To learn and know; and scarce was lit that flame
Of pleasure, whereof previous ignorance
In her young soul had dulled intelligence,
Than the enchaunting spell prevails no more,
And every brain is almost as before;
Almost I say, for there was slight mistake.   310
King Charles, forsooth, the sturdy sense must take
Of old Bonneau, who, for his part received
Wits of the monk; and thus were all deceived.
Little advantage came of this exchange;
The human reason, God's great gift, 't is strange,
Is a small thing, but grudgingly bestowed,
And every mortal's content with his load.
So change had with the lovers no effect;
Each one preserved for his fair dame elect
His former taste and sweet significance: 320
And what has love to do with common sense?
For Corisandre, new knowledge she procured

Of good and ill; a confidence assured
Of art and taste, an excellent reward
For all her previous innocence ignored;
All this the presents of a muleteer!
Thus Adam's silly partner, so we hear,
In garden lived and pleasure came not near,
Until the Devil hove within her sight,
And made her charming, subtile, witty, light,   330
As are the women whom to day we meet,
Who have no need the Devil to entreat.

LA PUCELLE

VARIANT OF CANTO XXI*

President Louvet falls sadly in love with the Lord Talbot —
The Maid with the ass of Denis.

　　Now must I tell what consequences sad
Conculix' most disgraceful conduct had;
What to audacious Tirconel befell,
What succour strange and salutary as well
Our Reverend friar was able to entreat
For Dorothy, and for the Sorel sweet,
And with what art he set them safe and free.
With what a fire and what dexterity,
Maid from Dunois was ravished by the ass,
And how God's vengeance on him came to pass,　　10
Who had, with Satan's help, defiled the Maid.
But before all, 't is Orléans siege arrayed,
Where many warriors brave clashed arms and fell,
'T is there we need to let our interest dwell.
O God of Love! O power by frailty known!
O fatal Love! how nearly hadst thou thrown
That citadel of France in hostile hands,
Success unhoped of those who hate our lands.
What Bedford, in experience grown old,
And Talbot sought to do, albeit bold,　　20

*This Canto having been entirely changed, we give it as it exists in the edition of twenty-four cantos, in which it forms the last Canto. [*Note from original edition.*]

161

And failed at last, O Love, thou wouldst attain!
Reader, reflect, their fatal flames of bane
Your bodies burn, and sore your souls beguile
Dear child! thou workest ruin with a smile.

In that sad land, while Love his arrows flings,
Where hundred heroes struggled for two Kings,
His tender hand, months since wrought grievous smart
On mighty Talbot with a golden dart,
That in the first of his two sheaves he found.
It was before that siege so long renowned,   30
An armistice, alas too short, they make;
Louvet and he, in peace their supper take;
This Louvet, president of worthy fame,
Was rash enough to bid to sup his dame.
Madame inclined somewhat to play the prude;
Wherefore Love thought her pride should be subdued.
For prudes he hates and oft will them abase.
Thus he deranged the sternness of her face,
Her noble dignity he changed indeed,
For certain traits which unto madness lead.   40
Dame President, on this auspicious day,
Great Talbot wins and charms his wits away.

You've seen already that grim escalade,
Assault of blood, and horrid cannonade,
Those brave attempts, and all those desperate fights,
Within, without, and on the ramparts' heights;
When Talbot and his fiery following train
The ramparts and the gates had burst and ta'en;
When on them from the houses' tops there broke
Sword, flame and grisly death at one fell stroke.   50
Then fiery Talbot, with his agile walk,
Tramples the dying, through the town to stalk,
He upset all things; crying out aloud:
"My Britons, enter and disarm the crowd!"
Much he resembled then to war's great god,
Beneath his footsteps echoing the sod,
When Discord and Bellona and high Fate,

As minister of Death arm him with hate.

Dame President within her walls a breach
That looked upon a ruined cot, could reach;   60
And through this hole her gallant could espy,
His golden helm, where feathers curl and fly,
His mailed arm, and those live sparks of flame,
Which from his pupils' orbits darting came,
That carriage proud, that demi-god's great air;
Dame President was almost in despair;
With shame dumbfounded and bereft of wits:
As once, when in her grated stage box sits
That erst famed beauty love has sore inflamed,
And ogles Baron, actor justly famed.   70
With ardent eyes she feasts upon his face,
His rich adornment, gestures and his grace,
Mingled with his her accents in tones low,
Love's flames received, her senses owned the glow.

Unable to resist, Dame President,
Consumed by passion, calls her confidant:
"Run, Suson, fly, and when you find him, say,
O bid him come and lead me hence away!
Convey to him, if him you can not find
That he take pity on my lot unkind;   80
That if he be a worthy, gallant knight,
I'll sup with him, within his house to-night."
The confidant dispatched a little page;
It was her brother; well he earned his wage;
With no delay six hardy lackeys call
At Louvet's house, and force the outer wall.

They enter and a woman masked they see,
Painted and patched, with many a coquetry,
Her hair or true or false raised to a bow,
On either side in curls was rayed below.   90
They take her up; she vanished from view,
By secret paths which the brave Talbot knew.

The handsome Talbot on that famous day
Through so much blood and fire had made his way,
That on the eve in dalliance with Love's charms,
He would forget the trouble of his arms.
Each mighty hero, though he win or lose,
To sup with a fair dame, would rather choose.
Thus Talbot, who has suffered no defeat,
Awaits within his house his lady sweet.   100

All things are ready for a supper fine;
The chased glass flagons of the rarest wine
Twixt lumps of cooling ice are there to tap,
Those liquid rubies, and that brilliant sap
Which Citeaux' blessed cellars hoard and hide;
In the proud tent, upon the other side,
A sofa, elegantly shaped, is placed,
Soft, low and wide, with proper fittings graced,
With back inclined, and two supports incased.
There our two lovers at their will could play;   110
Sir Talbot 'gan to live in the French way.

His care was first forthwith, the fair to find,
Who to his wooing had proved passing kind.
All things around him of his lady tell.
They bring her in, she's introduced as well.
A monster gray, in childish ruffs and frills,
Just three feet high, not to forget her heels.
Her little eyes with lively red ornate,
Yellow effusions ever inundate;
Her broad flat nose, twisted and turned within   120
Seems to drop straight upon her long hooked chin.

The Devil's mistress, Talbot thinks to take;
He utters cries at which the tables shake.
It was fat Louvet's sister whom had brought
The guard when in his house his wife they sought;
She strutted round with pride and pleasure spent
In rich delight at such a ravishment.

Dame President the direst grief assailed;
To think how her high enterprise had failed,
She quite lost heart at this misreckoning,   130
And cursed her sister like a Valois King.
Already love had troubled sore her wit,
'T was worse now jealousy had part in it,
Her troubled mind was lit with further flame,
And madder than before she now became.

More mad, the Ass once more to Joan returned;
The Maid was moved; her troubled senses yearned;
Her eyes on fire, "For Denis' sake!" cried she,
"Is it true, Sir, that you're in love with me?"
"In love with you? O, can you doubt it more?"   140
Replied the Ass! "You only I adore.
Heav'n! I was jealous of the Cordelier,
And served with pleasure when the squire was there,
Who saved you from the cloistered lust and rage,
Which the frocked beast endeavoured to assuage.
But jealous more a thousand times am I
Of the brute Dunois, fruit of bastardy!
With jealous anger drunk, with mad love fraught,
Dunois to Italy I did transport.
He came back weary, offered you his heart;   150
More handsome he, more amorous my part!
O noble Joan! thine age's prop and pride,
Whose maidenhead the world has glorified,
Is it Dunois' to play the victor's part?
It shall be I, I swear it by my heart!
Sure Heav'n removed she-asses from my way,
That mine embraces, pure for thee should stay!
If ever gentle, tender and discreet,
Until to-day I've kept my secret sweet,
If Joan be flattered my desires to greet,   160
If full of love, as ardent as it's true,
I Heavenly paths forsake, because of you;
If oft upon my back you've used to ride,
To bear me, in your turn, you might decide."

The Maiden this audacious suit received
With anger, which amazement sore retrieved;
And yet her mighty heart could but reflect
Some secret flattery at so strange effect,
Caused by her beauty signal and immense,
Upon so crass a soul's thick-witted sense,   170
She stretched her lily hand unto her swain,
With scarce a thought; then drew it back again.
She blushed afraid, condemns herself, alas!
Then reassured exclaims to him: "Fair ass,
Chimerical the hope you entertain;
Respect my duty and my glory's chain;
Too broad the diff'rences that us divide.
I never could your tenderness abide;
O, have a care and urge me not too far!"
The ass replied: "Love levels every bar.   180
Think of the swan by Leda not disdained,
Nathless an honest woman she remained.
Know you the daughter unto Minos born,
Who for a bull's sake heroes held in scorn,
And for her comely beast bore many a pain?
Know, by an eagle, Ganymede was ta'en,
How Philyra her lavish favours threw
On the sea-god, whom as a horse she knew."

The Devil, while thus he argued from his store,
The Devil, first author of all fabled lore,   190
Furnished him fresh examples for his case,
So that the Ass might take our *Savants'* place.
Joan listened: what can eloquence not teach?
The ear attack, if you the heart would reach;
Astonishment in sudden silence sinks.
Joan is confused, she wonders, dreams and thinks.
To love an ass and yield to him her pride!
There was dishonour she could not abide,
Who lived, her innocence preserved, to tell,
From muleteers and knights of France as well,   200
Who had, supported by high Heaven's grace,
In mortal fight brought Chandos to disgrace!

But this fair ass a gallant seems divine,
What hero, more than he, can sparkle, shine?
None could more tender be, nor show more wit;
Upon his back the Christ was wont to sit,
Eternal plains have ever been his place,
Of Seraphim he has the wings and face;
No bestiality in him abides,
Rather Divinity his aspect hides.   210

    Within her heart these thoughts a tempest formed,
And all her mind was troubled and deformed.
So on the ocean deep, one oft may spy
The haughty tyrants of the wave and sky,
One rushing from the distant Austral caves,
While one from icy Boreal regions raves,
Some wandering ship on Ocean to appal,
Seeking Ceylon, Sumatra or Bengal.
Anon the hull seems lifted to the sky,
Then near the rocks is hurried perilously;   220
Then comes the abyss with its engulfing swell,
Seeming to issue from the jaws of Hell.

    Thus is our Amazon in torment thrown;
The ass insisting, agitated Joan,
In her confusion, could not hold at all
That useful rudder which we reason call.
Her eyes are all ablaze with tender fire
Her senses reel, her heart admits desire;
Anon her face to sudden pallor grows,
Anon with lively blush it burns and glows.   230
A direful gesture of the orator,
More than all else was dangerous to her.
No longer o'er her senses is she queen;
Quite moist and languishing her eyes are seen.
Out of her bed her gracious head has slid,
In half closed eyes the shame she feels is hid,
Her charms robust are lavished to the view,
Bared are her buttocks' curves of swarthy hue;
She looks below, and wonders what she sees;

Bended beneath her are her pliant knees.   240
So we are told Thibouville and Villars,
Who imitated Caesar from afar,
Inflamed by the fire which was their fate,
With lowered heads would Nicomander wait,
And frequently with vigorous emprise
Their Picard lackeys' bodies fertilize.

The cunning boy who rules all things with rods,
The human race, donkeys as well as gods,
With bow in hand, in heights of Heaven stayed,
And with a smile of pleasure watched the Maid,   250
Twisting her rump and twining close her thighs,
Catching the fire with which her lover sighs,
Hasting the moment when her maid-hood dies.
Nor is her satin crupper loath to press
The bare sword of her ass with fond caress.

Three times the Maid, of maiden-hood relieved
Within her burning manor had received
The precious unction of the heavenly spring;
And times a four that point so menacing,
Within the fair to very quick had been.   260
To see is but to feel — so Joan had seen
The mighty fire within her person lit,
Spark after spark be born and die from it;
When suddenly she hears a voice that cries:
"Hasten, O Joan, your exploits signalize;
Rise ye at once, Dunois is under arms,
The fight is up, already our gendarmes
By the king's side to rally have begun;
Equip yourself, 't is time that sleep were done."

'T was Dorothy who spoke, the young, the fair,   270
By kind intent to Joan she'd hurried there;
Thinking to find her wrapped in slumber's arms,
She came to see, and hurry her to arms.
Thus crying to the Fair, who panted still,
She oped the door: the lock was fastened ill,

The twain were at their zenith as she came.
Three times she crossed herself for very shame.
Venus was less astounded, when of old
Webbed traps of steel were made her form to hold,
For all the gods and cuckold Vulcan too,   280
Naked with Mars above she met their view.
When Dorothy was recognized by Joan;
As seeing all, she lay as turned to stone;
Then turned to bed again, arranged the sheet,
Before she said, in tones as firm as sweet:
"My child, a mighty mystery you observe,
It is a vow, made for the King I serve:
And if appearances against me stalk,
I'm sorry for it — but you will not talk.
No limits I admit to friendship's right,   290
Yours is my silence in an equal plight;
Especially from Dunois hide this thing,
Or you might risk your country and your King."
So speaking, blithely leapt she from her bed,
Essence of lavender she lavished,
Breeches she took, a change of shift she made,
In cuirass and in arms was soon arrayed,
When Dorothy, still lost in her surprise,
Thus spoke to her with frankness in her eyes:
"Madam, in truth, my merely simple mind   300
Is little versed in exploits of this kind;
Your secret I will keep, I swear it so:
For bitter wounds of love, myself, I know;
Misfortune, touching me, has fully taught
To pardon harmless frailties as one ought.
All tastes I do respect, oh, pray believe!
But I confess, I hardly can conceive,
How when within one's arms one may embrace
Handsome Dunois, one can oneself abase,
Thus to reward the vile needs of an ass?   310
How can one bring oneself to such a pass
Or how submit oneself to the desires,
And attitude, which such a case requires?
I should be quite with consternation dazed,

Alarmed, beside myself and sore amazed,
At the mere thought of what the pain must be
In finding space for such enormity;
The stiffness and the unimagined strength
Of the destroying weapon, and its length;
In fine, how can you unresistingly,   320
Without disgust, quite conscientiously,
Have so small vanity, so little pride,
As thus to serve desires undignified?
The handsome Dunois for an ass to leave,
Hoping, withal, some pleasure to receive;
For pleasure you received, my beauteous Dame!
I read it in your eyes, your eyes of flame.
In me, at least, weak nature has her share;
I know myself, I should have too much fear
At such a swain." Then Joan, replying, said,   330
And sighed: "*Alas! had he loved you instead!*"

DECORATIONS:
IN VERSE AND PROSE

BEYOND.

Love's aftermath! I think the time is now
That we must gather in, alone, apart
The saddest crop of all the crops that grow,
      Love's aftermath.
Ah, sweet, — sweet yesterday, the tears that start
Can not put back the dial; this is, I trow,
Our harvesting! Thy kisses chill my heart,
Our lips are cold; averted eyes avow
The twilight of poor love: we can but part,
Dumbly and sadly, reaping as we sow,
      Love's aftermath.

IN VERSE

DE AMORE.

Shall one be sorrowful because of love,
    Which hath no earthly crown,
    Which lives and dies, unknown?
Because no words of his shall ever move
    Her maiden heart to own
    Him lord and destined master of her own:
Is Love so weak a thing as this,
    Who can not lie awake,
    Solely for his own sake,
For lack of the dear hands to hold, the lips to kiss,
        A mere heart-ache?

Nay, though love's victories be great and sweet,
    Nor vain and foolish toys,
    His crowned, earthly joys,
Is there no comfort then in love's defeat?
    Because he shall defer,
    For some short span of years all part in her,
    Submitting to forego
    The certain peace which happier lovers know;
Because he shall be utterly disowned,
    Nor length of service bring
    Her least awakening:
Foiled, frustrate and alone, misunderstood, discrowned,
        Is Love less King?

Grows not the world to him a fairer place,
    How far soever his days
    Pass from his lady's ways,
From mere encounter with her golden face?
    Though all his sighing be vain,
    Shall he be heavy-hearted and complain?
Is she not still a star,
Deeply to be desired, worshipped afar,
    A beacon-light to aid
    From bitter-sweet delights, Love's masquerade?
Though he lose many things,
    Though much he miss:
The heart upon his heart, the hand that clings,
    The memorable first kiss;
Love that is love at all,
Needs not an earthly coronal;
Love is himself his own exceeding great reward,
       A mighty lord!

Lord over life and all the ways of breath,
    Mighty and strong to save
    From the devouring grave;
Yea, whose dominion doth out-tyrant death,
    Thou who art life and death in one,
    The night, the sun;
Who art, when all things seem:
    Foiled, frustrate and forlorn, rejected of to-day,
    Go with me all my way,
And let me not blaspheme.

THE DEAD CHILD.

Sleep on, dear, now
    The last sleep and the best,
And on thy brow,
    And on thy quiet breast,
Violets I throw.

Thy scanty years
    Were mine a little while;
Life had no fears
    To trouble thy brief smile
With toil or tears.

Lie still, and be
    For evermore a child!
Not grudgingly,
    Whom life has not defiled,
I render thee.

Slumber so deep,
    No man would rashly wake;
I hardly weep,
    Fain only, for thy sake,
To share thy sleep.

Yes, to be dead,
　Dead, here with thee to-day, —
When all is said
　'Twere good by thee to lay
My weary head.

The very best!
　Ah, child so tired of play,
I stand confessed:
　I want to come thy way,
And share thy rest.

CARTHUSIANS.

Through what long heaviness, assayed in what strange fire,
　　Have these white monks been brought into the way of peace,
Despising the world's wisdom and the world's desire,
　　Which from the body of this death bring no release?

Within their austere walls no voices penetrate;
　　A sacred silence only, as of death, obtains;
Nothing finds entry here of loud or passionate;
　　This quiet is the exceeding profit of their pains.

From many lands they came, in divers fiery ways;
　　Each knew at last the vanity of earthly joys;
And one was crowned with thorns, and one was crowned with bays,
　　And each was tired at last of the world's foolish noise.

It was not theirs with Dominic to preach God's holy wrath,
　　They were too stern to bear sweet Francis' gentle sway;
Theirs was a higher calling and a steeper path,
　　To dwell alone with Christ, to meditate and pray.

A cloistered company, they are companionless,
　　None knoweth here the secret of his brother's heart:
They are but come together for more loneliness,
　　Whose bond is solitude and silence all their part.

O beatific life! Who is there shall gainsay,
    Your great refusal's victory, your little loss,
Deserting vanity for the more perfect way,
    The sweeter service of the most dolorous Cross.

Ye shall prevail at last! Surely ye shall prevail!
    Your silence and austerity shall win at last:
Desire and mirth, the world's ephemeral lights shall fail,
    The sweet star of your queen is never overcast.

We fling up flowers and laugh, we laugh across the wine;
    With wine we dull our souls and careful strains of art;
Our cups are polished skulls round which the roses twine:
    None dares to look at Death who leers and lurks apart.

Move on, white company, whom that has not sufficed!
    Our viols cease, our wine is death, our roses fail:
Pray for our heedlessness, O dwellers with the Christ!
    Though the world fall apart, surely ye shall prevail.

THE THREE WITCHES.

All the moon-shed nights are over,
 And the days of gray and dun;
There is neither may nor clover,
 And the day and night are one.

Not an hamlet, not a city
 Meets our strained and tearless eyes;
In the plain without a pity,
 Where the wan grass droops and dies.

We shall wander through the meaning
 Of a day and see no light,
For our lichened arms are leaning
 On the ends of endless night.

We, the children of Astarte,
 Dear abortions of the moon,
In a gay and silent party,
 We are riding to you soon.

Burning ramparts, ever burning!
 To the flame which never dies
We are yearning, yearning, yearning,
 With our gay and tearless eyes.

In the plain without a pity,
 (Not an hamlet, not a city)
 Where the wan grass droops and dies.

VILLANELLE OF THE POET'S ROAD.

Wine and woman and song,
  Three things garnish our way:
Yet is day over long.

Lest we do our youth wrong,
  Gather them while we may:
Wine and woman and song.

Three things render us strong,
  Vine leaves, kisses and bay;
Yet is day over long.

Unto us they belong,
  Us the bitter and gay,
Wine and woman and song.

We, as we pass along,
  Are sad that they will not stay;
Yet is day over long.

Fruits and flowers among,
  What is better than they:
Wine and woman and song?
  Yet is day over long.

VILLANELLE OF ACHERON.

By the pale marge of Acheron,
   Methinks we shall pass restfully,
Beyond the scope of any sun.

There all men hie them one by one,
   Far from the stress of earth and sea,
By the pale marge of Acheron.

'Tis well when life and love is done,
   'Tis very well at last to be,
Beyond the scope of any sun.

No busy voices there shall stun
   Our ears: the stream flows silently
By the pale marge of Acheron.

There is the crown of labour won,
   The sleep of immortality,
Beyond the scope of any sun.

Life, of thy gifts I will have none,
   My queen is that Persephone,
By the pale marge of Acheron,
   Beyond the scope of any sun.

SAINT GERMAIN-EN-LAYE.

[1887-1895]

Through the green boughs I hardly saw thy face,
They twined so close: the sun was in mine eyes;
And now the sullen trees in sombre lace
Stand bare beneath the sinister, sad skies.

O sun and summer! Say in what far night,
The gold and green, the glory of thine head,
Of bough and branch have fallen? Oh, the white
Gaunt ghosts that flutter where thy feet have sped,

Across the terrace that is desolate,
And rang then with thy laughter, ghost of thee,
That holds its shroud up with most delicate,
Dead fingers, and behind the ghost of me,

Tripping fantastic with a mouth that jeers
At roseal flowers of youth the turbid streams
Toss in derision down the barren years
To death the host of all our golden dreams.

AFTER PAUL VERLAINE.

I.

Il pleut doucement sur la ville.
RIMBAUD.

Tears fall within mine heart,
As rain upon the town:
Whence does this languor start,
Possessing all mine heart?

O sweet fall of the rain
Upon the earth and roofs!
Unto an heart in pain,
O music of the rain!

Tears that have no reason
Fall in my sorry heart:
What! there was no treason?
This grief hath no reason.

Nay! the more desolate,
Because, I know not why,
(Neither for love nor hate)
Mine heart is desolate.

AFTER PAUL VERLAINE.

II.

COLLOQUE SENTIMENTAL.

Into the lonely park all frozen fast,
Awhile ago there were two forms who passed.

Lo, are their lips fallen and their eyes dead,
Hardly shall a man hear the words they said.

Into the lonely park, all frozen fast,
There came two shadows who recall the past.

'Dost thou remember our old ecstasy?' —
'Wherefore should I possess that memory?' —

'Doth thine heart beat at my sole name alway?
Still dost thou see my soul in visions?' 'Nay!' —

'They were fair days of joy unspeakable,
Whereon our lips were joined?' — 'I cannot tell.' —

'Were not the heavens blue, was not hope high?' —
'Hope has fled vanquished down the darkling sky.' —

So through the barren oats they wanderèd,
And the night only heard the words they said.

AFTER PAUL VERLAINE.
III.

SPLEEN.

Around were all the roses red,
The ivy all around was black.

Dear, so thou only move thine head,
Shall all mine old despairs awake!

Too blue, too tender was the sky,
The air too soft, too green the sea.

Always I fear, I know not why,
Some lamentable flight from thee.

I am so tired of holly-sprays
And weary of the bright box-tree,

Of all the endless country ways;
Of everything alas! save thee.

AFTER PAUL VERLAINE.

IV.

The sky is up above the roof
    So blue, so soft!
A tree there, up above the roof,
    Swayeth aloft.

A bell within that sky we see,
    Chimes low and faint:
A bird upon that tree we see,
    Maketh complaint.

Dear God! is not the life up there,
    Simple and sweet?
How peacefully are borne up there
    Sounds of the street!

What hast thou done, who comest here,
    To weep alway?
Where hast thou laid, who comest here,
    Thy youth away?

TO HIS MISTRESS.

There comes an end to summer,
 To spring showers and hoar rime;
His mumming to each mummer
 Has somewhere end in time,
And since life ends and laughter,
 And leaves fall and tears dry,
Who shall call love immortal,
 When all that is must die?

Nay, sweet, let's leave unspoken
 The vows the fates gainsay,
For all vows made are broken,
 We love but while we may.
Let's kiss when kissing pleases,
 And part when kisses pall,
Perchance, this time to-morrow,
 We shall not love at all.

You ask my love completest,
 As strong next year as now,
The devil take you, sweetest,
 Ere I make aught such vow.
Life is a masque that changes,
 A fig for constancy!
No love at all were better,
 Than love which is not free.

JADIS.

Erewhile, before the world was old,
When violets grew and celandine,
In Cupid's train we were enrolled:
      Erewhile!
Your little hands were clasped in mine,
Your head all ruddy and sun-gold
Lay on my breast which was your shrine,
And all the tale of love was told:
Ah, God, that sweet things should decline,
And fires fade out which were not cold,
      Erewhile.

IN A BRETON CEMETERY.

They sleep well here,
 These fisher-folk who passed their anxious days
 In fierce Atlantic ways;
And found not there,
 Beneath the long curled wave,
 So quiet a grave.

And they sleep well
 These peasant-folk, who told their lives away,
 From day to market-day,
As one should tell,
 With patient industry,
 Some sad old rosary.

And now night falls,
 Me, tempest-tost, and driven from pillar to post,
 A poor worn ghost,
This quiet pasture calls;
 And dear dead people with pale hands
 Beckon me to their lands.

TO WILLIAM THEODORE PETERS
ON HIS RENAISSANCE CLOAK.

The cherry-coloured velvet of your cloak
    Time hath not soiled: its fair embroideries
Gleam as when centuries ago they spoke
    To what bright gallant of Her Daintiness,
      Whose slender fingers, long since dust and dead,
    For love or courtesy embroidered
The cherry-coloured velvet of this cloak.

Ah! cunning flowers of silk and silver thread,
    That mock mortality! the broidering dame,
The page they decked, the kings and courts are dead:
    Gone the age beautiful; Lorenzo's name,
      The Borgia's pride are but an empty sound;
    But lustrous still upon their velvet ground,
Time spares these flowers of silk and silver thread.

Gone is that age of pageant and of pride:
    Yet don your cloak, and haply it shall seem,
The curtain of old time is set aside;
    As through the sadder coloured throng you gleam;
      We see once more fair dame and gallant gay,
    The glamour and the grace of yesterday:
The elder, brighter age of pomp and pride.

THE SEA-CHANGE.

Where river and ocean meet in a great tempestuous frown,
Beyond the bar, where on the dunes the white-capped rollers break;
Above, one windmill stands forlorn on the arid, grassy down:
I will set my sail on a stormy day and cross the bar and seek
That I have sought and never found, the exquisite one crown,
Which crowns one day with all its calm the passionate and the weak.

When the mad winds are unreined, wilt thou not storm, my sea?
 (I have ever loved thee so, I have ever done thee wrong
In drear terrestrial ways.) When I trust myself to thee
With a last great hope, arise and sing thine ultimate, great song
Sung to so many better men, O sing at last to me,
That which when once a man has heard, he heeds not over long.

I will bend my sail when the great day comes; thy kisses on my face
Shall seal all things that are old, outworn; and anger and regret
Shall fade as the dreams and days shall fade, and in thy salt embrace,
When thy fierce caresses blind mine eyes and my limbs grow stark
            and set,
All that I know in all my mind shall no more have a place:
The weary ways of men and one woman I shall forget.

Point du Pouldu.

DREGS.

The fire is out, and spent the warmth thereof,
 (This is the end of every song man sings!)
The golden wine is drunk, the dregs remain,
Bitter as wormwood and as salt as pain;
And health and hope have gone the way of love
Into the drear oblivion of lost things.
Ghosts go along with us until the end;
This was a mistress, this, perhaps, a friend.
With pale, indifferent eyes, we sit and wait
For the dropt curtain and the closing gate:
This is the end of all the songs man sings.

A SONG.

All that a man may pray,
　　Have I not prayed to thee?
What were praise left to say,
　　Has not been said by me,
　　　　O, ma mie?

Yet thine eyes and thine heart,
　　Always were dumb to me:
Only to be my part,
　　Sorrow has come from thee,
　　　　O, ma mie?

Where shall I seek and hide
　　My grief away with me?
Lest my bitter tears should chide,
　　Bring brief dismay to thee,
　　　　O, ma mie?

More than a man may pray,
　　Have I not prayed to thee?
What were praise left to say,
　　Has not been said by me,
　　　　O, ma mie?

BRETON AFTERNOON.

Here, where the breath of the scented-gorse floats through the sun-
        stained air,
On a steep hill-side, on a grassy ledge, I have lain hours long and heard
Only the faint breeze pass in a whisper like a prayer,
And the river ripple by and the distant call of a bird.

On the lone hill-side, in the gold sunshine, I will hush me and repose,
And the world fades into a dream and a spell is cast on me;
And what was all the strife about, for the myrtle or the rose,
And why have I wept for a white girl's paleness passing ivory!

Out of the tumult of angry tongues, in a land alone, apart,
In a perfumed dream-land set betwixt the bounds of life and death,
Here will I lie while the clouds fly by and delve an hole where my
        heart
May sleep deep down with the gorse above and red, red earth beneath.

Sleep and be quiet for an afternoon, till the rose-white angelus
Softly steals my way from the village under the hill:
Mother of God, O Misericord, look down in pity on us,
The weak and blind who stand in our light and wreak ourselves such ill.

VENITE DESCENDAMUS.

Let be at last; give over words and sighing,
    Vainly were all things said:
Better at last to find a place for lying,
    Only dead.

Silence were best, with songs and sighing over;
    Now be the music mute;
Now let the dead, red leaves of autumn cover
    A vain lute.

Silence is best: for ever and for ever,
    We will go down and sleep,
Somewhere beyond her ken, where she need never
    Come to weep.

Let be at last: colder she grows and colder;
    Sleep and the night were best;
Lying at last where we can not behold her,
    We may rest.

TRANSITION.

A little while to walk with thee, dear child;
    To lean on thee my weak and weary head;
Then evening comes: the winter sky is wild,
    The leafless trees are black, the leaves long dead.

A little while to hold thee and to stand,
    By harvest-fields of bending golden corn:
Then the predestined silence, and thine hand,
    Lost in the night, long and weary and forlorn.

A little while to love thee, scarcely time
    To love thee well enough; then time to part,
To fare through wintry fields alone and climb
    The frozen hills, not knowing where thou art.

Short summer-time and then, my heart's desire,
    The winter and the darkness: one by one
The roses fall, the pale roses expire
    Beneath the slow decadence of the sun.

EXCHANGES.

All that I had I brought,
   Little enough I know;
A poor rhyme roughly wrought,
   A rose to match thy snow:
All that I had I brought.

Little enough I sought:
   But a word compassionate,
A passing glance, or thought,
   For me outside the gate:
Little enough I sought.

Little enough I found:
   All that you had, perchance!
With the dead leaves on the ground,
   I dance the devil's dance.
All that you had I found.

TO A LADY ASKING FOOLISH QUESTIONS.

Why am I sorry, Chloe? Because the moon is far:
And who am I to be straightened in a little earthly star?

Because thy face is fair? And what if it had not been,
The fairest face of all is the face I have not seen.

Because the land is cold, and however I scheme and plot,
I can not find a ferry to the land where I am not.

Because thy lips are red and thy breasts upbraid the snow?
(There is neither white nor red in the pleasance where I go.)

Because thy lips grow pale and thy breasts grow dun and fall?
I go where the wind blows, Chloe, and am not sorry at all.

RONDEAU.

Ah, Manon, say, why is it we
Are one and all so fain of thee?
Thy rich red beauty debonnaire
In very truth is not more fair,
Than the shy grace and purity
That clothe the maiden maidenly;
Her gray eyes shine more tenderly
And not less bright than thine her hair,
　　Ah, Manon, say!
Expound, I pray, the mystery
Why wine-stained lip and languid eye,
And most unsaintly Maenad air,
Should move us more than all the rare
White roses of virginity?
　　Ah, Manon, say!

MORITURA.

A song of the setting sun!
   The sky in the west is red,
And the day is all but done:
    While yonder up overhead,
      All too soon,
There rises, so cold, the cynic moon.

A song of a winter day!
   The wind of the north doth blow,
From a sky that's chill and gray,
    On fields where no crops now grow,
      Fields long shorn
Of bearded barley and golden corn.

A song of an old, old man!
   His hairs are white and his gaze,
Long bleared in his visage wan,
    With its weight of yesterdays,
      Joylessly
He stands and mumbles and looks at me.

A song of a faded flower!
   'Twas plucked in the tender bud,
And fair and fresh for an hour,
    In a lady's hair it stood.
      Now, ah, now,
Faded it lies in the dust and low.

LIBERA ME.

Goddess the laughter-loving, Aphrodite befriend!
Long have I served thine altars, serve me now at the end,
Let me have peace of thee, truce of thee, golden one, send.

Heart of my heart have I offered thee, pain of my pain,
Yielding my life for the love of thee into thy chain;
Lady and goddess be merciful, loose me again.

All things I had that were fairest, my dearest and best,
Fed the fierce flames on thine altar: ah, surely, my breast
Shrined thee alone among goddesses, spurning the rest.

Blossom of youth thou hast plucked of me, flower of my days;
Stinted I nought in thine honouring, walked in thy ways,
Song of my soul pouring out to thee, all in thy praise.

Fierce was the flame while it lasted, and strong was thy wine,
Meet for immortals that die not, for throats such as thine,
Too fierce for bodies of mortals, too potent for mine.

Blossom and bloom hast thou taken, now render to me
Ashes of life that remain to me, few though they be,
Truce of the love of thee, Cyprian, let me go free.

Goddess, the laughter-loving, Aphrodite, restore
Life to the limbs of me, liberty, hold me no more.
Having the first-fruits and flower of me, cast me the core.

TO A LOST LOVE.

I seek no more to bridge the gulf that lies
    Betwixt our separate ways;
    For vainly my heart prays,
Hope droops her head and dies;
I see the sad, tired answer in your eyes.

I did not heed, and yet the stars were clear;
    Dreaming that love could mate
    Lives grown so separate; —
But at the best, my dear,
I see we should not have been very near.

I knew the end before the end was nigh:
    The stars have grown so plain;
    Vainly I sigh, in vain
For things that come to some,
But unto you and me will never come.

WISDOM.

Love wine and beauty and the spring,
   While wine is red and spring is here,
And through the almond blossoms ring
   The dove-like voices of thy Dear.

Love wine and spring and beauty while
   The wine hath flavour and spring masks
Her treachery in so soft a smile
   That none may think of toil and tasks.

But when spring goes on hurrying feet,
   Look not thy sorrow in the eyes,
And bless thy freedom from thy sweet:
   This is the wisdom of the wise.

IN SPRING.

See how the trees and the osiers lithe
Are green bedecked and the woods are blithe,
The meadows have donned their cape of flowers,
The air is soft with the sweet May showers,
    And the birds make melody:
But the spring of the soul, the spring of the soul,
    Cometh no more for you or for me.

The lazy hum of the busy bees
Murmureth through the almond trees;
The jonquil flaunteth a gay, blonde head,
The primrose peeps from a mossy bed,
    And the violets scent the lane.
But the flowers of the soul, the flowers of the soul,
    For you and for me bloom never again.

A LAST WORD.

Let us go hence: the night is now at hand;
    The day is overworn, the birds all flown;
    And we have reaped the crops the gods have sown;
Despair and death; deep darkness o'er the land,
Broods like an owl; we cannot understand
    Laughter or tears, for we have only known
    Surpassing vanity: vain things alone
Have driven our perverse and aimless band.

Let us go hence, somewhither strange and cold,
    To Hollow Lands where just men and unjust
    Find end of labour, where's rest for the old,
Freedom to all from love and fear and lust.
Twine our torn hands! O pray the earth enfold
Our life-sick hearts and turn them into dust.

IN PROSE

THE FORTUNATE ISLANDS.

Bearded, with tawny faces, as they sat on the quay, looking listlessly at nothing with their travelled eyes, I questioned them:

'We have adventured,' they said.

'Tell me of your travels, O mariners, of that you have sought and found, of high perils undergone and great salvage and of those fortunate islands which lie in a quiet sea, azure beyond my dreaming.'

'We have found nothing. There is nothing saved,' they said.

'But tell me, O mariners, for I have travelled a little. I have looked for the woman I might have loved, and the friend we hear of, and the country where I am not. Tell me of your discoveries.'

One of them answered:

'We tell you the truth. We are old, withered mariners, and long and far have we wandered in the seas of no discovery. We have been to the end of the last ocean, but there was nothing, not even the things of which you speak. We have adventured, but we have not found anything, and here we are again in the port of our nativity, and there is only one thing we expect. Is it not so, comrades?'

Each raised a hand of asseveration; and they said:

'We tell you the truth: there are no fortunate islands.'

And they fell into their old silence.

209

MARKETS.

AFTER AND OLD NURSERY RHYME.

'Where are you going, beautiful maiden?'

'I am going to market, sir.'

'And what do you take with you, beautiful maiden? Lilies out of your garden? White milk, warm from the cow, little pats of yellow butter, new-laid eggs, this morning's mushrooms? Where is your basket? Why have you nothing in your hands?'

'I am going to market, sir.'

'Beautiful maiden, may I come with you?'

'Oh, sir.'

ABSINTHIA TAETRA.

Green changed to white, emerald to an opal: nothing was changed.

The man let the water trickle gently into his glass, and as the green clouded, a mist fell away from his mind.

Then he drank opaline.

Memories and terrors beset him. The past tore after him like a panther and through the blackness of the present he saw the luminous tiger eyes of the things to be.

But he drank opaline.

And that obscure night of the soul, and the valley of humiliation, through which he stumbled were forgotten. He saw blue vistas of undiscovered countries, high prospects and a quiet, caressing sea. The past shed its perfume over him, to-day held his hand as it were a little child, and to-morrow shone like a white star: nothing was changed.

He drank opaline.

The man had known the obscure night of the soul, and lay even now in the valley of humiliation; and the tiger menace of the things to be was red in the skies. But for a little while he had forgotten.

Green changed to white, emerald to an opal: nothing was changed.

THE VISIT.

As though I were still struggling through the meshes of some riotous dream, I heard his knock upon the door. As in a dream, I bade him enter, but with his entry, I awoke. Yet when he entered it seemed to me that I was dreaming, for there was nothing strange in that supreme and sorrowful smile which shone through the mask which I knew. And just as though I had not always been afraid of him I said: 'Welcome.'

And he said very simply, 'I am here.'

Dreaming I had thought myself, but the reproachful sorrow of his smile showed me that I was awake. Then dared I open my eyes and I saw my old body on the bed, and the room in which I had grown so tired, and in the middle of the room the pan of charcoal which still smouldered. And dimly I remembered my great weariness and the lost whiteness of Lalage and last year's snows; and these things had been agonies.

Darkly, as in a dream, I wondered why they gave me no more hurt, as I looked at my old body on the bed; why, they were like old maids' fancies (as I looked at my gray body on the bed of my agonies) — like silly toys of children that fond mothers lay up in lavender (as I looked at the twisted limbs of my old body), for these things had been agonies.

But all my wonder was gone when I looked again into the eyes of my guest, and I said:

'I have wanted you all my life.'

Then said Death (and what reproachful tenderness was shadowed in his obscure smile):

'You had only to call.'

THE PRINCESS OF DREAMS.

Poor legendary princess! In her enchaunted tower of ivory, the liberator thought that she awaited him.

For once in a dream he had seen, as they were flowers de luce, the blue lakes of her eyes, had seemed to be enveloped in a tangle of her golden hair.

And he sought her through the countless windings of her forest for many moons, sought her through the morasses, sparing not his horses nor his sword. On his way he slew certain evil magicians and many of his friends, so that at his journey's end his bright sword was tarnished and his comeliness swart with mud. His horses he had not spared; their bones made a white track behind him in the windings of the forest: but he still bore her ransom, all the costly, graceful things stored in a cypress chest: massed pearls and amethysts and silks from Samarcand, Valance of Venice, and fine tapestry of Tyre. All these he brought with him to the gates of her ivory tower.

Poor legendary princess.

For he did not free her and the fustian porter took his treasure and broke his stained sword in two.

And who knows where he went, horseless and disarmed, through the morasses and the dark windings of her forest under the moonless night, dreaming of those blue lakes which were flowers de luce, her eyes ? Who knows? For the fustian porter says nothing, being slow of wit.

But there are some who say that she had no wish to be freed, and that those flowers de luce, her eyes, are a stagnant, dark pool, that her glorious golden hair was only long enough to reach her postern gate.

Some say, moreover, that her tower is not of ivory and that she is not even virtuous nor a princess.

NOTES

Those poems listed under *Verses* or *Decorations* are first published there unless we specifically mention an earlier publication. Likewise with manuscripts, we list all the manuscript versions we are aware of, rather than say repeatedly when there are none known to us. The information in the annotations is usually in the following order:

1. Identification of dedicatee, if known.
2. Previous printings before *Verses* and *Decorations*.
3. Manuscripts.
4. Significant corrections or variations.
5. Explanatory or additional notes.

POÉSIE SCHUBLADE

p.9: **To Cynara**
Flower notebook, front endpaper.
Line 9 was originally: 'Thou loved'st me once ah woe is me I love thee'.

p.10: **A Mosaic**
Flower notebook, pp.2-3.
Dowson spent some of his childhood in Italy.

p.11: **Requiem**
Flower notebook, pp.4-5.

p.12: **Potnia Thea**
Flower notebook, pp.5-7, dated 'Aug. 1886'.

The 'dread goddess' of the Greek title is Anangke or Necessity. She was the mother of Clotho, Lachesis and Atropos, the three Fates, or Parcae (to give them their Roman name), who respectively weave, measure and cut off the thread of life. Dowson sees her as surviving all other gods. Zeus, son of Cronos, has gone; Aphrodite, who first stepped ashore at Cythera, but the centre of whose cult was subsequently Paphos, has gone; Athene, who had guarded Athens, whose citizens had seen Theseus sail in the Delian barque to kill the Minotaur on Crete, has gone; Hera, Zeus's queen on Olympus, has gone; Hephaestus, the lame smith-god, son of Zeus and Hera, whose forges were under Etna, has gone with all the other heroes; the holy sites on the mountains of Cithaeron where Dionysus, sometimes called Bromius, was ecstatically worshipped, are silent. But Anangke remains — Necessity or Fate personified.

p.14: **Rondeau: 'Could you forget'**

Flower notebook, pp.7-8.

p.15: **Rondeau: 'In Autumn'**

Flower notebook, p.8.

In the notebook, Dowson marks that the form is missing a line after line 11. On the facing page he tries out the line 'Ah sweet howbeit thy heart doth wear' but deletes it. He then crosses out firmly the last five lines, finally making a light cross through the whole poem. In line 2 he tries 'dead' and 'calm' before settling on 'still'.

p.16: **Sonnets, I, In Memoriam. H.C.**

Flower notebook, p.9.

We cannot identify the friend to whom Dowson refers here.

p.17: **Sonnets, II, Novalis**

Flower notebook, p.10.

'Novalis' was the pseudonym of Friedrich Leopold von Hardenberg (1772-1801), German Romantic poet and novelist. In his early twenties he formed a passionate attachment to Sophie von Kühn, a beautiful but delicate girl of thirteen, and gained the consent of her and her parents to marry when she came of age. She died two years later. He died of tuberculosis before his planned marriage to a new love. Although the quotation has the spirit of Novalis's *Hymnen an die Nacht*, it has been impossible to identify it in his works.

p.18: **Sonnets, Of a Little Girl, (i)**

Flower notebook, p.11.

p.19: **Sonnets, Of a Little Girl, (ii)**
Flower notebook, p.12.

p.20: **Sonnets, Of a Little Girl, (iii)**
Flower notebook, p.13.
Dowson corrects 'faith' to 'hope' in 1.4 and 'stilly' to 'quietly' in 1.8.

p.21: **Sonnets, Of a Little Girl, (iv)**
First printed in *London Society*, vol. 50, November 1886, over the initials
E. C. D. Flower notebook, p.14, dated '1885', with the note 'published
London Society'.

p.22: **Sonnets, Of a Little Girl, (v)**
Flower notebook, p.15.

p.23: **Sonnets, Of a Little Girl, (vi)**
Flower notebook, pp.15-16.

p.24: **Sonnets, Of a Little Girl, (vii)**
Flower notebook, pp.16-17.

p.25: **Sonnets, Of a Little Girl, (viii): Epilogue**
First published in the *Savoy*, no. 7, November 1896, p.87; and in
Decorations as 'A Last Word'.
Flower notebook, p.17.
Flower printed the poem twice in *Poetical Works*, once in the sequence
of sonnets in the notebook and under its new title 'A Last Word' as the
last poem in *Decorations*. We take his hint, but seize the opportunity to
publish here the version of the poem as it was first written, and note
the changes that developed it into the poem as it finally appeared.
The first four lines were more or less set from the start, except that
darkness was 'on the land' in 1.4. He corrected 'Broods for all time' to
'Broods every day', but the next six lines show a remarkable increase
in strength. He first changed 'all that is shown / Is bitter to the core,
while overthrown' to 'all that is shown / Surpasseth bitterness, the die
is thrown'. On the opposite page he built further on this with new
lines to follow 'we cannot understand': 'Laughter or tears or love, for
we have known, / Surpassing vanity: vain things alone / Have driven
our perverse and foolish band.' He further corrected 'Let us go hence,
the grave is doubtless cold, / The coffin dark' to 'Let us go hence to
somewhere dark and cold / To hollow lands'. The final changes for
publication can be seen on p.207.

p.26: **La Jeunesse n'a qu'un Temps**
Flower notebook, p.18. The title means 'youth comes only once'.

p.27: **Song of the XIXth Century**

Flower notebook, p.19.

p.28: **A Lullaby**

Flower notebook, pp.19-20.

p.29: **Spleen**

Flower notebook, pp.20-21.

The poem ran over two pages and Dowson scored through the three stanzas on the first page, leaving the last four as possibly a separate poem.

p.31: **After Many Years**

Flower notebook, pp.22-23.

p.33: **Praeterita**

Flower notebook, pp.24-25.

The Latin title means 'things gone by, passed over; the past'.

p.35: **Adios!**

Flower notebook, pp.28-29.

p.36: **Seraphita-Seraphitūs**

Flower notebook, pp.30-31.

The angelic Séraphîtüs-Séraphîta features in Honoré de Balzac's *Séraphita*, of 1834-6, a Swedenborgian romance. This androgynous and mysterious figure is loved by Wilfrid who thinks of her as a woman and by Minna who thinks of him as a man. The figure represents the love that unites them. Dowson's interest may have been stimulated by Charles Morice's mention of *Séraphita* as Balzac's nearest approach to art in *La Littérature de tout-à-l'heure* of 1889 (p.167).

p.37: **It is finished**

Flower notebook, p.33.

The title quotes Christ's last words on the cross; from John, 19, 30.

p.38: **Ere I go Hence**

Flower notebook, p.34.

The form is almost a collection of Rondelets, as if Dowson is experimenting with the styles described by Gleeson White in his *Ballades and Rondeaus* (1887).

p.39: **Transit Gloria**

Flower notebook, pp.35-37, dated 'May.19.1887.'

The phrase 'sic transit gloria mundi' ('Thus passes away the glory of this world') is from Thomas à Kempis, *Imitatio Christi*, ch.3, §vi.

The correction of ll.11-12 from 'Too bitter for pleasure, / Too gentle for pain' scarcely disguises the Swinburnean influence.

p.42: **Sonnet To Nature: Morituri te salutant**

Flower notebook, p.38, dated 'Aug.1887.' Published in *London Society* in March 1888.

The salutation of the gladiators – 'We who are about to die salute you' – is used by Suetonius in his *Life of Claudius*, 21.

Dowson changed 'cold' to 'wild' in l.3.

p.43: **Awakening**

Flower notebook, pp.39-40, dated 'May.1888.'

Dowson changed 'pleasure' to 'knowledge' in l.22.

p.44: **Lullaby**

Flower notebook, pp.40-41, dated 'May. 1888.' and with the note 'Rejected – Atalanta'.

Dowson suggested 'hallow' for 'Light up' in l.10 but did not decide.

p.45: **The Old Year**

Flower notebook, pp.42-3, dated at the end '31/12/88.'

p.47: **The New Year**

Flower notebook, pp.44-5, dated at the end 'Jan 1889.'

Dowson takes away some of the more archaising language of his original. In ll.9ff. he corrects from 'Being passing weary of the sun? / Will there be one of them shall gain, / Ay, even one'; and in l.13 he corrects from 'Nay, ask not that'.

p.48: **From the Icelandic**

Flower notebook, pp.45-7, dated 'April 1889' and with a pencil note on the opposite page: 'Rejected — Temple Bar'

The original title was 'Thalassios', perhaps after Swinburne's poem 'Thalassius' in *Songs of the Springtides* (1880).

Dowson's revisions in the manuscript tend to take away the more medievalising element: 'Long time ago' in l.1 replaces 'When I was young'; 'daedal' in l.5 replaces 'smiling'; 'bitter' in l.12 replaces 'sad sweet'; 'Was it not this' in l.26 replaces 'Nay was't not this'; 'Waited and yearned for' in l.27 replaces 'And waited for yearned for'; 'Ah lean thy brow over me, shroud my face' of l.31 replaces 'Ah cover me, lull me, enshroud my face'. There is no evidence of an Icelandic original, and it seems uncharacteristic of Icelandic poetry.

p.50: **Love's Epilogue**

Flower notebook, pp.49-50, dated 'Aug 2: 1889', with note 'Rejected

— English Illustrated, Chambers Journal'.

p.52: **Rondeau: Hélène**

Flower notebook, p.52, dated 'Aug.1889.'

We do not know if there was a real Hélène to whom Dowson dedicated this poem. Given Dowson's liking for fixed poetic forms, this poem could have been inspired by Ronsard, whose famous *Sonnets pour Hélène* (1578) were dedicated to a lady-in-waiting of Catherine de'Medici. Dowson may also have derived inspiration and information from Gleeson White's anthology of poems in fixed forms, called (to give it its full title) *Ballades and Rondeaus, Chants Royal, Sestinas, Villanelles, &c. Selected, with Chapter on the Various Forms* (1887), of which he possessed a copy (see notes to 'A Letter to M.M.' below). This volume would provide him with examples of rondeaus, roundels, rondels, villanelles, and triolets at which he must have been tempted to try his hand. This poem and the next conform to what White calls (arbitrarily as he admits) roundels. Dowson's use is near to Swinburne's version in his *A Century of Roundels* (1883), though he does not rhyme the refrain line with the second rhyme. Dowson might have been intrigued by Arthur Symons's effort at a roundel which White includes, with its Dowsonesque theme:

> If rest is sweet at shut of day
> For tired hands and tired feet,
> How sweet at last to rest for aye,
> If rest is sweet.

p.53: **Roundel: To Hélène**

Flower notebook, p.54, dated 'Oct. 27th. 89'.

Lethe, the river of oblivion, is one of the streams of Hades, whose waters caused those who drink to forget their former existence. Nepenthe is a drug, mentioned in the *Odyssey*, capable of banishing grief or trouble.

p.54: **Rondel**

Flower notebook, p.56, dated at the end 'Feb. 4. '90'.

Gleeson White's *Ballades and Rondeaus* says that 'With Charles d'Orléans the rondel took the distinct shape we now assign to it, namely, of fourteen lines on two rhymes, the first two lines repeating for the seventh and eighth, and the final couplet. . . . In this, the true type of the rondel, the two-lined refrain occurring three times in its fourteen makes it an unwieldy form to handle' (p.lviii).

p.55: 'Because my life is an unworthy thing' (Discedam, explebo . . .)

Flower notebook, p.69, dated 'Jan 31. '91'.

The Latin epigraph, added in pencil to the ms, comes from *Aeneid* VI, ll.545-6. The lines are the farewell of the ghost Deiphobus to Aeneas at the end of their meeting in the underworld: 'I shall go, I shall fill up the number, I shall be given back to the darkness. Go, our glory, go. And I wish you better luck'.

Dowson introduced this sonnet to his friend Sam Smith in a letter of about the same date: 'I have just read through the VIth Aeneid; and am intoxicate with its adorable phrases. After all with all our labours of the file and chisel we can not approach these people, in this gross tongue. — "Sunt lacrimae rerum et mentem mortalia tangunt" [*Aeneid* I, l.462: "Here there are tears to flow and human hearts to feel for human woe"] — "Umbrarum hic locus est Somni Noctisque soporae," [*Aeneid* VI, l.390: "This is the place of shades, of sleep and of drowsy night"] —

Discedam, explebo numerum reddarque tenebris.

I, decus, I nostrum; melioribus utere fatis."

On to the last couplet, by the way, I have tagged a sonnet' (*Letters*, pp.181-2). Dowson then adds a footnote to say that the sonnet is 'Entitled "To a Child growing out of Childhood: and Away!" (a real Hobby Horse title, I swear.[)]'

The opening of line 12 has been corrected from 'In flowery ways' and the last line corrects the original rather weak: 'Until the harvest is all harvested'.

p.56: Against My Lady Burton

Flower notebook, pp.85-86; dated at the end 'Nov. 10th. 1891'.

Sir Richard Burton (1821-1890) was the celebrated linguist, explorer, anthropologist and translator. He published accounts of his travels, poetry, books on folklore and volumes of scholarship and erotica. Shortly after his death on 20th October 1890, his wife Isabel destroyed his newly-revised version of *The Scented Garden*. Perhaps to compensate for the actual problems of their marriage, Isabel wrote a hagiographic account of her husband, and burned all his papers so there is little evidence on which to base a fuller and truer picture. She told *The Morning Post* in June 1891 that she had burned it in the interests of her husband's soul.

Dowson may not have known that the Burtons were married in 1861 in the Bavarian Church in which Adelaide was to marry; but he perhaps knew that Smithers had been involved in the publication of some of Burton's erotic works and was no doubt aware when Smithers published Burton's translation of the *Carmina* of Catullus in 1894, which Isabel had savagely purged.

EARLY AND UNCOLLECTED POEMS

p.57: **A Letter from M.M. versified out of poor prose into catchpenny verse!**
Manuscript: Written by Dowson on p.213 (the otherwise blank page announcing 'Triolets') of his copy of Gleeson White's *Ballades and Rondeaus*, 1887, which was no.247 in the Elkin Matthews-A.J.A.Symons catalogue, where the poem is described as translated by Dowson from an unpublished triolet in Latin or Greek by Lionel Johnson.

The comment by Johnson on the quality of periodicals of the day was no doubt stimulated by the snubbing of his work, perhaps by Mowbray Morris (1847-1911), the editor of *Macmillan's Magazine*, although more likely by the editor of *Murray's Magazine*, W.L.Courtney (1850-1928), former Fellow of New College Oxford and later editor of the *Fortnightly Review*, who in October 1890 had rejected something of Johnson's. Dowson reported to Arthur Moore that 'Johnson was very furious the other night, having just been rejected by his "own familiar" tutor, Courtney of "Murrays"' (*Letters*, p.175). In the same letter, Dowson reiterates the spirit of the verse when he says: 'I have made an endeavour to-day to read the Philoktetes; compassing about 50 lines; it's a distinct grind but I think necessary, if one is not altogether to lose the habit of Greek'. Augustine Birrell (1850-1933) was known for his light-hearted wit and humour, most notably in his two volumes of essays, *Obiter Dicta* (1884-87). Birrell was a lawyer from 1875 and a Liberal member of the House of Commons (1889-99, 1906-18).

p.57: **'In the days of the good, gay people'**
Manuscript: Originally written in a copy of *The Pierrot of the Minute* with the inscription: 'For Miss Ida Baltye | This piece of moonshine | With the hommage of the author | Ernest Dowson'. The leaf, torn from the book, was no.209 in the Elkin Mathews-A.J.A. Symons Catalogue.

p.58: **The Passing of Tennyson**
First printed in *T.P.'s Weekly* in 1915 and reprinted in the *Literary Digest*,

27 March 1915, and again in *Known Signatures* (1932), pp.36-7.

Manuscript: None, but related papers in No 68 MS Walpole 19 in the Bodleian Library.

This poem came to light when it was discovered by Edwin B. Hill of Ysleta, Texas. The original was destroyed by fire but a copy was preserved and discovered by Hill in 1934. The Bodleian letter reads:

> Dear Mr Symons
>
> After many years! ... In a sad copy of Browning, this morning, I found the enclosed 'item' so vainly sought. I am certain not half a dozen are in existence, as my papers were lost or burned sixteen years ago when I left Arizona.
>
> How fares the First Editions Club and its publications?
>
> Faithfully,
>
> Edwin B. Hill
>
> 5 July 1934

Dowson wrote to Plarr on 8 October 1892: 'I am sorry that Tennyson has crossed the bar: if only, that it leaves us so much at the mercy of Sir Edwin, L. Morriss, Austin et Cie. But he was un grand poète, tout de même. Above all I love him because he did sacredly hate the mob — which whether it be the well dressed mob whom Browning pandered to, or the evil smelling mob to which William Morris does now still, to the detriment of his art and the offence of his own dignity still pander, I hold alike to be damnable, unwholesome and obscene.' (*Letters*, p.243). The poem 'In Autumn' is appended to this letter to Plarr.

The references to Bedivere (a variant spelling of Bedevere) are to the knight of the Arthurian legends who was responsible for carrying out the dying King Arthur's wish to throw Excalibur into the lake and for bearing Arthur's body to the barge which took him to Avalon, his final resting place. The Mantuan is Virgil, in his capacity as a guide, as in Dante's *Divine Comedy*.

p.59: Fantaisie Triste

First printed in *Known Signatures*, ed. John Gawsworth (1932), p.35.

Manuscript: The MS was no.206 in the Elkin Mathews-A. J. A. Symons catalogue. We take our text corrected from the MS now in the Berg Collection of New York Public Library. The manuscript deletes 'Of Autumn' as the fourth line of stanza 2.

VERSES

Verses was published by Leonard Smithers in June 1896 in an edition of 300 Small Paper Copies on handmade paper and 30 Large Paper Copies on Japanese vellum. The binding, with a design by Beardsley in gold, was of white Japanese vellum. Dowson thought the book 'a very dainty little white book' (*Letters*, p.368) and sent his compliments to Smithers 'on the luxury with which you have encadré my lucubrations. The cover is really very beautiful: and I congratuate Beardsley if, as I gather, his is the design' (*Letters*, p.365). He wrote also to Sam Smith to ask 'Do you like Aubrey Beardsley's binding-block? I am very pleased with it' (*Letters*, p.366). Beardsley's design is splendidly elegant and spare and seems to summarize the basic structure of many other of his drawings; and his reported explanation of the Y shape — that it was a comment on the verses asking 'Y were they ever written?' — seems a smart riposte rather than a considered opinion. The book was printed by the Chiswick Press.

A book of poems by Dowson had been announced in the *Bookman* of November 1893 as forthcoming from the Bodley Head in 1894, and Dowson's *Dilemmas* (1895) had described as 'IN PREPARATION / (Uniform with Selwyn Image's Poems and Carols) / BY THE SAME AUTHOR / A VOLUME OF POEMS'. His book would have fitted well with Image's book and Herbert Horne's *Diversi Colores*, and Dowson is referring to his change in plan when he writes to Plarr that 'I am afraid Horne is annoyed with me because I have published my verses out of the series' (*Letters*, p.362). Dowson's account in a letter to John Gray of 27 December 1895, says that 'At present the delay is due chiefly to the fact that I am unable to make up my mind with whom to publish them. I do not feel particularly bound to Mathews, as the arrangement was made, so long ago, and not directly with me, and he could have published them two years ago if he had wished, but he professes to be very anxious now to have them. And the fact of his having advertized them makes it difficult for me to give them to Smithers, as I should like to do, as besides offering me most magnificent terms, he is one of my most intimate friends'. He chose to publish with Smithers, whose support was so important to him in the ensuing years.

p.63: **Vitae summa brevis spem nos vetat incohare longam**
The title is from Horace's *Odes* I, iv, 15, where the poet, reminded by

the return of Spring, warns Sestius that 'the short span of our life forbids us to indulge in a long-term hope'.

p.65: **In Preface: for Adelaide**

Adelaide is of course Ellen Adelaide Mary Foltinowicz, the 'Missie' of the dedication to *Dilemmas* and Dowson's lifelong ideal love. She was the daughter of a Polish coffee house keeper, born on the thirteenth of April 1878 at 19 Sherwood Street, Soho, above the family business. She was thus eighteen when the book was published. A year later, on the 26th of September 1897, she married Augustus Noelte in the Bavarian Chapel, Westminster. The marriage certificate gives the place of residence for both as 19 Sherwood Street, and describes both the groom and the fathers of bride and groom as tailors. Adelaide died in Sherwood Street on 13 December 1903 as the result of a botched abortion.

Dowson's original intention for the dedication was to have no identification. He wrote to Sam Smith that 'I hope the dedication of my poems will be understood of her and accepted — as, although there is no name, nor initials even, it will doubtless be understood of others — who will not, I hope, think it extravagant. It is very literally true' (*Letters*, p.358). He worried that the Preface might be 'indiscreet' but, in spite of Smith's reservations about it, he added her name. 'Perhaps you are right in your remarks about my preface', he wrote to Smith. 'Conal is dedicating to me his new novel "A Fool and his Heart" and I fear the dedication is appropriate. But it is too late to convert me now; I am idolatrous for the rest of my days. Idolatrous to the extent that Keats was when he wrote from Rome to his friend Browne: "the lining which she put in my travelling cap *scalds* my head", — and like Keats I can not open her letters for a day or so after they reach me' (*Letters*, p.367).

The quotation in French is from Flaubert's *Education sentimentale*.

p.67: **A Coronal**

Manuscripts: 1. In Flower notebook, pp.64-5, dated 'Oct 16th 90', with the title 'A Dedication: with His poems and Her Days to His Lady; and to Love', and with the note 'Rejected: Longmans Mag.' 2. In a letter to Plarr of 5 March 1891.

In the letter to Plarr (*Letters*, pp.187-8) Dowson is considering possible titles for a book of poems they were planning. He is looking for a 'harmonious' one and prefers 'Vineleaf and Violet' or 'Rose and Pine'. If they choose the former title, he says, 'perhaps the appended perfectly meaningless verses would come in', adding that this was 'the only poem that I ever wrote straight off in less than an hour'. There are few corrections: 'Perfumed' replaces 'Fragrant' in l.5; 'night' for 'eve' in l.7; 'blossoms' for 'flowers' in l.15; and in l.25 he tries 'we sorrowfully lay' and 'At fall of night we lay' before settling on 'At set of sun we lay'. Although Symons reports that Dowson's 'ideal of a line of verse' was Poe's 'The viol, the violet, and the vine' and that he had a theory that 'the letter "v" was the most beautiful of all the letters and could never be brought into verse too often', there are few occasions which bear that out, of which this is the most obvious example.

p.69: **Nuns Of The Perpetual Adoration**

We cannot identify the Countess Sobieska von Platt.

First published in the *Century Guild Hobby Horse*, vol VI, 1891, p.136 with 'Flos Lunae' and 'Amor Umbratilis' under the general title 'In Praise of Solitude'. Published with a French translation by Henry Davray in the *Mercure de France* of March 1892. Published in the first *Book of the Rhymers' Club* (1892), p.10.

Manuscripts: 1. Lionel Johnson's copy of the Rhymers' book has some manuscript alterations. 2. Flower manuscript, pp.72-3, dated 'Feb 10. 1891' and annotated 'Hobby Horse April 1891'. 3. A copy said to be in the collection of Michael Holland. 4. A copy in Queen's College Oxford.

It was earlier called '(The) Carmelite Nuns of the Perpetual Adoration' and 'Ursulines of the Perpetual Adoration'.

Opposite the poem in the Flower notebook, he has written 'Procul o procul este profani' ('Hence, o hence, you that are uninitiated'), a quotation from *Aeneid* VI, l.258.

In l.7 'lives' replaces 'hours' and the magnificent l.14 replaces the original 'The sound of laughter, and of wild despair'. In l.30 'choice' replaces 'part' and in the last line 'beside' replaces 'beneath'. The most striking corrections are to the fifth stanza, which originally read:

> The roses of the world, they knew, shall fade,
>> And be trod under by the hurrying feet:
> They saw the glory pageant of the world displayed;
>> They saw the bitter did outweigh the sweet.

Lines 27-28 had first read:

> Mary's sweet Star shines on them through the night,
>> And lightens them in lone security.

p.71: **Villanelle of Sunset:**

First published in the *Book of the Rhymers' Club* (1892), p.83.

Flower notebook, p.62, dated 'June 2/1890'. Not divided into stanzas until *Verses*.

The 'white bird' of line 7 is rather oddly 'robin' in the first draft.

p.72: **My Lady April**

Léopold Nelken was a Polish medical student, who became Dowson's closest friend in Paris in the years 1895-6 and seems to have been as generous, improvident and dissolute as Dowson himself. Dowson describes him in a letter to Arthur Moore written over Christmas 1895: 'I have made one great friend here, a Russian — or rather a Pole — though most of his people live in Petersburg — by name Leopold Nelken — a most charming fellow studying medicine here. Like all Russians he has been everywhere & speaks all languages & like the best kind of Russian he has that sort of indefinable 'Varsity quality which is lacking in most of my French acquaintances' (*Letters*, p.336). In January 1896 he wrote to Conal O'Riordan that 'I avoid everybody, except Leopold Nelken, who is awfully nice to me' (*Letters*, p.341).

First published in *Temple Bar*, vol LXXXV, part 341, April 1889, p.514.

Flower notebook, p.32, dated 'April. 1888', and called 'Sonnet/ April'.

Dowson typically moderates his language away from the 'poetic' in l.8, which originally read: 'Of tears her drooping lashes are not bare'. He also characteristically substitutes 'vanity' for 'misery' in the penultimate line.

p.73: **To One in Bedlam**

Henry Davray (1873-1944), French author, Hon. Sec. of the Anglo-French Society, and journalist on the *Mercure de France* where he was for many years chief reviewer of English books; he reviewed *Verses* there in August 1896. Davray was a frequent correspondent of Dowson and was a point of call in Paris for many young English writers and artists. He published translations of Dowson's 'My Lady April' and 'Villanelle of Marguerites' in *La Revue Sentimentale* in July 1896, and was planning to translate 'To One in Bedlam' and 'Sapientia Lunae' for the *Mercure de France*. The translations never appeared, though Dowson's letter to Davray of June 1896 explaining phrases in the latter two poems survives (*Letters*, p.370). Dowson explains that the scentless wisps of straw 'is a rather fantastic image (I imagine the madman . . . making imaginary bouquets of roses out of the straw which lines his cage)'.

First published in the *Albemarle*, vol. II, no.2, August 1892; reprinted in *The Second Book of the Rhymers' Club* (1894), p.34.

p.74: **Ad Domnulam Suam**

First published in the *Book of the Rhymers' Club* (1892), p.53.

Manuscripts: 1. Flower notebook, pp.66-7, dated 'Oct 18th 1890.'; 2. In a letter to Arthur Moore of 19 October 1890 (*Letters*, p.173), where Dowson comments: 'A mere trifle - pardon it - who can have inspired it?' (He had met Adelaide by November 1889).

Dowson's difficulties with the title in the Flower notebook — whether to call it 'Ad Domnulae Meae' or 'Ad Domnulam Suam' — help to indicate the origin of the title in Walter Pater's *Marius the Epicurean*. Pater writes of Marcus Aurelius's would-be apathy breaking down on the sickness or death of his children and quotes from Aurelius: 'On my return to Lorium . . . I found my little lady — domnulam meam — in a fever' (*Marius the Epicurean*, chapter XIII). Dowson often referred to Adelaide as his 'little lady'.

p.75: **Amor Umbratilis**

First published in the *Century Guild Hobby Horse*, vol VI, October 1891, p.137, along with 'Nuns of the Perpetual Adoration' and 'Flos Lunae' under the general title of 'In Praise of Solitude'. Republished in the *Book of the Rhymers' Club* (1892), p.41.

Manuscripts: 1. Flower notebook, pp.63-4, dated 'Sept 18th. 1890'; 2. On the back of a money-lender's letter, dated 7 October 1890; 3. In a letter to Arthur Moore dated 16-17 September 1890 (*Letters*, p.167).

In the letter to Moore, Dowson asks for criticism and wonders if Moore can provide a title. He also asks whether 'unobservant' is legitimate, and where he should try to place the poem. The Flower notebook has pencilled in that it was 'Rejected "English Illustrated" / Accepted "Century Guild Hobby Horse" / Oct 10th. 1890. / Pub. C. G. H. H. Oct. 1891 / & / Book of Rhymers Club 1892'. When he was considering the possibility of accepting Lionel Johnson's suggestion that a general title might be 'Umbratilia', which would have made his final title repetitive, he suggested 'Sola Beatudo' as an alternative.

The word 'umbratilis' comes from Pater's *Marius the Epicurean*, chapter II, where Pater describes the contemplative idealistic youth of Marius: 'Had the Romans a word for *unworldly*? The beautiful word *umbratilis* perhaps comes nearest to it; and, with that precise sense, might describe the spirit in which he prepared himself for the sacerdotal function hereditary in his family — the sort of mystic enjoyment he had in the abstinence, the strenuous self-control and *ascêsis*, which such preparation involved'.

p.76: **Amor Profanus**

Gabriel de Lautrec (1867-1938) was one of Dowson's circle of friends in France. He was an author and journalist, at one time leading contributor to *Le Courrier Français* and therefore a useful contact. Dowson obviously felt that Lautrec would help to spread his fame in France and sent him a copy of *Verses* and of his novel.

Even in what purports to be a *carpe diem* poem, the wistful negatives are stronger than the positives of the 'Profane love' of the title. Lalage appears in Horace's *Odes*, for example in I, xxii, where he says that wherever he may be set, he 'will love his sweetly smiling, sweetly speaking Lalage'.

p.78: **Villanelle of Marguerites**

We cannot identify a Miss Eugénie Magnus.

First published in *Temple Bar*, May 1894.

Manuscript on the rear endpaper of the Flower notebook numbered both 17 and 87A and dated 'Dec 31st 91'.

The 'snowy' petals of l.2 were originally 'rosy' and in l.14 'Kissed by' replaces 'Sings to'. The quoted phrase is a translation of the French way of telling fortunes by plucking the petals of daisies, the petals signifying in turn 'un peu, passionément, pas du tout'.

p.79: **Yvonne of Britanny**

Marmaduke Langdale was an actor in Sir Frank Benson's company and wrote occasional verse. He was a regular correspondent and Dowson writes of him as 'the faithful Marmie' (*Letters*, p.328). He is said to be the original for Archie Longdale in *Adrian Rome*, where he is cast as Captain Romilly in Rome's play. His 'appropriate soldier-like aspect was justified by his history (he had never regretted exchanging from a marching regiment, while his military fame was still as insignificant as his pay, into the histrionic ranks)' (*Adrian Rome*, Methuen, London, 1899, p.197).

p.81: **Benedictio Domini**

Selwyn Image (1849-1930), ordained priest in 1873, resigned his curacy of St. Anne's Soho in 1880 to devote himself religiously to art and architecture. He co-founded the Century Guild, whose magazine *The Century Guild Hobby Horse* and its successor *The Hobby Horse* published some of Dowson's pieces, including 'Non sum qualis eram'. His only book of poems was *Poems and Carols*, an exquisite little volume of 1894 (republished with an introduction by Woodstock Books in 1995). He became Slade Professor of Fine Art at Oxford in 1910, and his letters and a book of his poems were published by A. H. Mackmurdo in 1932.

First printed in *The Hobby Horse*, no. 3, 1894. Submitted for the *Second Book of the Rhymers' Club*, but withdrawn because publication would clash with the delayed *Hobby Horse* (see *Letters*, pp.295-6).

The subject of the poem, the benediction of God and the sanctuary of the church, is appropriate to its dedicatee. The subject relates closely to Dowson's experience of Notre Dame de France, the French Roman Catholic Church off Leicester Square. Dowson wrote a letter to Arthur Moore on 19 October 1890 in which he writes that 'You ought to have come to N.D. de France tonight. There was a procession after Vespers of the Enfants de Marie and I just managed to discern my special Enfant in spite of her veil, carrying a very big banner and looking as usual extremely self-possessed and mistress of the situation. It was a wonderful and beautiful situation: the church — rather dark the smell of incense — the long line of graceful little girls all with their white veils over their heads — banners —: a few sad faced nuns — and last of all the priest carrying the Host, vested in white — censed by an acolyte who walked backwards — tossing his censer up "like a great gilt flower": and to come outside afterwards — London again — the sullen streets and the sordid people of Leicester Square!' (*Letters*, p.172). He mentions Lionel Johnson in the same letter, and Johnson dedicated a poem on 'Our Lady of France' to Dowson (written in 1891, published in 1895), the first two lines of which are:

Leave we awhile without the turmoil of the town;
Leave we the sullen gloom, the faces full of care.

p.82: **Growth**

First published in the *Second Book of the Rhymers' Club* (1894), p.83.

Flower proposes quite reasonably that this is the poem on which Dowson was working at the time he was writing an extensive letter to Sam Smith about his feelings for Adelaide in April 1893 (*Letters*, pp.277-280).

p.83: **Ad Manus Puellae**

Leonard Smithers (1861-1907) publisher and staunch supporter of Dowson. Born in Sheffield, and initially a solicitor, he moved into the London bookselling and publishing world and published work which shocked, by being either avant-garde or pornographic or both. He supported and published Symons, Wilde and Beardsley as well as Dowson, and also published the *Savoy*. Wilde described him to Reginald

Turner in a letter of 10 August 1897, concluding with comments which explain his attraction for Dowson: 'He loves first editions, especially of women: little girls are his passion. He is the most learned erotomaniac in Europe. He is also a delightful companion, and a dear fellow, very kind to me' (*The Letters of Oscar Wilde*, edited by Rupert Hart-Davis, 1962, p.631). Wilde asked Smithers to put some flowers on Dowson's grave for him (*Ibid*, p.816).

Manuscripts: 1. In a letter to John Gray dated 24 February 1893 (*Letters*, pp.271-2); 2. in a letter to John Lane of February / March 1893 (*Letters*, pp.273-4, though the poem is not transcribed there).

The Latin title ('To the hands of a girl') is amplified in the Lane letter with a quotation from Verlaine: 'Rêves bénis, mains consacrées, | O ces mains, ses mains vénérées!' (Blessed dreams, sacred hands, O these hands, her worshipped hands!'). Flower's notes draw attention also to Flaubert and to Keats's 'Sonnet — to a Lady seen for a few moments at Vauxhall'; but pale, ivory and lily hands are well known in literature, especially in the medieval period which Dowson seems to wish to suggest with his language here.

In the letter to Gray, Dowson has the alternative title 'Ad Manus Dominae' ('To his Mistress' Hands') and the penultimate line reads: 'I am always in prison to their commands —'.

p.84: **Flos Lunae**

Yvanhoé Rambosson (1872-1943), minor French poet, author of *Le Verger Doré* (1895). A Paris friend of Dowson and Davray.

First published in *The Century Guild Hobby Horse*, vol. VI, October 1891, p.136, as part of a set of three (see above under 'Nuns of the Perpetual Adoration').

Manuscripts: 1. Flower notebook, p.79, where it is annotated 'Century Guild Hobby Horse' and dated 'July 20th. 1891'; 2. In a letter to Arthur Moore dated 'July 20/91', now in the Morgan Library, ms MA,1489-2 (*Letters*, pp.207-8); 3. In B.M. Add. MS 45135.

Dowson seemed undecided whether to render 'Flower of the moon' in French or Latin: it is 'Claire: la lune!' in Flower notebook, and 'Fleur de la lune' in the other mss. Perhaps the classicising influence of the *Hobby Horse* set decided him on the Latin.

In sending this to Moore, Dowson described it as 'the last vagary of my most modern Muse — of Montparnasse — or should I say Montmartre? Its obscurity, I may remark is designed' (*Letters*, p.208).

The Flower notebook has for line 14: 'Maid O maid of the lunar night' corrected from the version which appeared in the *Hobby Horse* and the letter to Moore: 'Pale daughter of the lunar night'.

p.85: **Non sum qualis eram bonae sub regno Cynarae**

First published in *The Century Guild Hobby Horse*, vol. VI, 1891, p.67, and in the *Second Book of the Rhymers' Club* (1894), p.60.

Manuscripts: 1. Flower notebook, pp.70-1, dated 'Feb. 7th. 1891', and annotated 'Hobby Horse – April 1891'; 2. In a letter to Arthur Moore of 7 February 1891 now in the Berg collection.

The title is from Horace's *Odes*, IV, I, 3, where Horace begs Venus not to make him enter her lists because 'I am not the man I was under kind Cynara's rule'. He tries to persuade her that the younger Paullus Maximus would be a more appropriate champion, but nonetheless he feels the old allegiance to her sway.

Dowson recognised the daring of this his most famous poem. He wrote to Sam Smith in March 1891 that 'I have seen the proofs of my "Cynara" poem for the April Hobby. It looks less indecent in print, but I am still nervous! Though I admire Horne's audacity. I read it, or rather Lionel did for me, at the last Rhymers' (*Letters*, p.190).

It is perhaps to the poem's appearance in the *Century Guild Hobby Horse* that we owe the moving of the notebook's exclamation mark at the end of the line to its place after 'Cynara' and other changes in punctuation. Very little was in fact revised. The 'kisses' in l.3 were originally 'roses'. Line 5 had 'grew desolate' instead of 'was desolate' and most surprisingly, 'in my fashion' began as 'after my fashion'. In the second stanza, 'mine heart' was 'my breast' in the Moore copy, and in the third stanza, 'all the time' replaces a repetition of 'desolate' presumably to avoid repetition of the effect in the first stanza. The second line of the last stanza has most variation. Dowson tried 'But when the cups are empty' and 'But when the viols are silent' before his choice of 'But when the feast is finished' in the Flower notebook, and he corrected 'lights' to 'lamps' in Moore's letter. Flower's note that the letter to Arthur Moore does not contain the last stanza is incorrect.

p.86: **Vanitas**

Vincent O'Sullivan (1868-1940), of a rich American Catholic family, was a congenial companion in the 1890s for Dowson and Smithers, and a benefactor of Wilde after the latter's release from gaol. Elkin Mathews published his *Poems* in 1896, Smithers published his book of weird and fantastic tales *A book of bargains* in 1896, and his poems *The houses of sin* (1897). He published *Aspects of Wilde* in 1936, but died in poverty in Paris in 1940. His *Opinions* were published in 1959. *Poems* and *The houses of sin* were reprinted with an introduction by Woodstock Books in 1995.

First published in the first *Book of the Rhymers' Club* (1892), p.69.

Flower notebook p.74, dated 'March 19/ 91'. Opposite is written in pencil: '"On my eyelids is the shadow of Death" Job xvi. 16'.

The bay and the laurel were symbolic of victory or poetic prowess, the palm of triumph, and the cypress of mourning. Flower and Maas propose that it is 'Vanitas' which Dowson sends in a letter to Plarr of 20 March 1891, describing them as 'my latest Versicles: the merest "symbolism", almost too slight for criticism! Its an attempt at mere sound verse, with scarcely the shadow of a sense in it: or hardly that so much as a vague, Verlainesque emotion. Its an inferior production' (*Letters*, p.189). Flower points justifiably to a strong influence of Swinburne's 'Garden of Proserpine', but as usual Dowson modifies Swinburne's enthusiastic cadences to his own dying fall.

p.87: **Exile**

Conal Holmes O'Connell O'Riordan (1874-1948) was born in Dublin and became an actor, publishing books under the pseudonym Norreys Conell and succeeding J. M. Synge as Director of the Abbey Theatre in Dublin in 1909. His *A Fool and his Heart* (1896) was dedicated to Dowson (see above under 'In Preface: for Adelaide').

Manuscripts: BM Add. MS. 45135, dated 9 May 1892 (*Letters*, pp.232-3), where Dowson says he has not 'yet contrived a title for it'.

The phrase 'water of separation' occurs in Numbers, 19, but with a different meaning. Dowson's meaning here is nearer to the 'weary river' of 'Vanitas'

p.88: **Spleen**

Arthur Symons (1865-1945), influential avant-garde poet and critic of the movements of the 1890s, Symbolism and Decadence, student of the seven arts, and an enthusiast for continental ideas and their introduction into England. His books of poetry, *Silhouettes* (1892) and *London Nights* (1895 and 1897), epitomise the 1890s. He edited the *Savoy*, and he wrote (among many other books of poetry, travel and criticism) the influential *The Symbolist Movement in Literature* (1900). Symons edited Dowson's poems in 1905, basing his introduction on the article on Dowson he had first published in the *Savoy* in August 1896. Dowson varied in his opinion of Symons: in November 1895, in a letter to Edgar Jepson, he said that 'He is (*don't show this to anyone*) — a silly b — r'

(*Letters*, p.319); in April 1896, he wrote to Davray that he found *Silhouettes* 'disappointing' (p.356); in January of 1898 he wrote to William Theodore Peters that Symons 'is very friendly and you are wrong in your impression of him' (p.403); in 1896, he responded to a draft of Symons' article by saying he was 'fortunate in my chronicler' (p.371). Desmond Flower, defending Dowson's memory from the picture that Symons gives of him, calls Symons 'one of the nastiest men I have ever met' (*New Letters from Ernest Dowson*, 1984, p.iii).

The poem is not a translation, which would have been appropriate for Symons, although Baudelaire in *Les fleurs du mal* and Verlaine in *Romances sans paroles* wrote poems with this title, one of which was translated both by Dowson in *Decorations* and by John Gray in *Silverpoints*.

p.89: ***O mors! quam amara est memoria tua homini pacem habenti in substantiis suis***

First published in the first *Book of the Rhymers' Club* (1892), p.30

Manuscripts: 1. Flower notebook, p.76, dated '28/April/91'; 2. A leaf in the A. J. A. Symons collection (Elkin Mathews catalogue, no 202); 3. A leaf in Arthur Moore's collection, now Pierpont Morgan Library ms MA.1489-1, dated '28/4/91'; 4. BM Add. MS 45135, dated April 28.91.

As often seems to be the case, it is the end of the poem which Dowson takes most care over. The last line was 'For one day!' in the BM ms, and 'This last day!' in the Rhymers' Club book.

The title is taken from Ecclesiasticus, 41, 1, which is rendered: 'O death, how bitter is the remembrance of thee to a man that liveth at rest in his possessions'. On the reverse of the Morgan Library ms MA.1489-1, Dowson has made a rough pencil draft of a triolet which seems a comic translation of this:

> think of
> To ~~remember~~ thee, O death
> very
> How / bitter 'tis
> For him who pondering [?] plies
> His peaceful biz
> For him who peaceful plies
> His   biz
> And battens on his biz

p.90: **'You would have understood me, had you waited'**

First printed in the *Second Book of the Rhymers' Club* (1894), p.120.

Flower notebook, pp.83-4, dated 'Sept 13th. 1891'.

The epigraph, which was added later to the ms without attribution, is from Verlaine: 'In these gloomy sojourns, nevers are evermores'. The lines are ll.11-12 of 'Réversibilités' from *Parralèlement* (1889). Dowson changes 'ywis, I was' to 'in truth was I' in l.11, and 'grave' to 'mound' in l.23.

p.92: April Love

Arthur Cecil Hillier (1857-1914). Plarr introduced Dowson to Hillier, who was one of the Irish members of the Rhymers' Club. Dowson's reference to Hillier in a letter of 8 April 1890 as 'Hillier of Worcester and the New YorKerald' suggests that their Oxford careers may have overlapped in 1886, in which year Hillier graduated from Worcester College. He had graduated from Trinity College Dublin in 1878, and was now London Correspondent of the *New York Herald*, and in 1890 went with Dowson to Brittany. He was a member of the Rhymers' Club and was the major collaborator with G.A.Greene and Dowson in translating Muther's *History of Modern Painting* (1895-6). He also collaborated with Greene in a serialised novel *The Lost Prima Donna*. Marion Plarr in *Cynara* (1933) writes of '"Poor" Hillier, who was in a mad asylum' (p.208).

p.93: Vain Hope

Manuscript: BM Add MS 45135, where its title is 'The Gate of Ivory'. In Latin mythology, there are two sets of gates in the Underworld: through the gates of horn pass the dreams that are to come true and through the gates of ivory pass the dreams that are sent to deceive mortals.

p.94: Vain Resolves

Flower notebook pp.86-7, dated 'Dec. 3rd 1891'.

'I will fasten me' in l.14 replaces 'I pass presently' and 'passed' in l.15 replaces 'stopped'.

p.95: A Requiem

John Gray (1866-1934) encapsulates the 1890s struggle between the worldly and the religious/idealistic. His *Silverpoints* (1893) is an exquisite icon of the period with its consciously decadent air, while his *Spiritual poems* (1896) explore religious themes. A disciple of Wilde in the early 1890s, he renounced that world to become a Roman Catholic priest in Edinburgh, where with the help of his lifelong friend André Raffalovich, he built St Peter's, where he was parish priest until his death. In the early 1890s he was a close friend of Dowson and a frequent visitor to 'Poland', the restaurant where Adelaide lived.

First printed in *The Hobby Horse*, no.3, 1894.

Horace's love-sick and dissatisfied Neobule (*Odes*, III, xii) seems a more lively young woman than Dowson's.

p.96: **Beata Solitudo**

Sam Smith (1867-1938) was a good friend and faithful correspondent of Dowson from his Oxford days, where Smith studied law at Queen's (1886-1890). Smith taught for ten years in preparatory schools before going to Enfield Grammar School where he remained until retirement in 1931. His (anonymous) translation of *Lysistrata* was illustrated by Beardsley and published by Smithers in 1896.

Perhaps the dedication of a poem on 'Blessed solitude' is an ironic comment on Dowson's occasional wish to avoid Smith's company.

p.98: **Terre Promise**

Herbert Percy Horne (1864-1916) so impressed his instructor, A. H. Mackmurdo, that he was taken as a full partner in the Century Guild, where Horne gradually became full editor of the *Century Guild Hobby Horse*, until it ceased in 1892, and then editor of its brief successor, the *Hobby Horse*, in 1893-4. Horne was architect, book-designer, editor, poet, art collector and art critic, and wrote a well-respected book on Botticelli. His scholarship and bearing gave him an authority with the young writers of the day who often gathered at his house, 20 Fitzroy Street, and he was helpful in Dowson's early career. Dowson gives a delightful portrait of Horne and Image in a letter of 27 January 1890: 'In the evening I slacked & eventually met Image & Horne at midnight outside the "back door" of the Alhambra! & was introduced to various trivial coryphées. There was something eminently grotesque in the juxtaposition. Horne very erect & slim & aesthetic — & Image the most dignified man in London, a sort of cross in appearance between a secular abbé & Baudelaire, with a manner du 18me siècle — waiting in a back passage to be escort to ballet girls whom they don't even — !!! I confess this danseuse-worship escapes me!! Horne seems a man of merit however' (*Letters*, p.132). Horne attended Dowson's funeral. His *Diversi Colores* (1891) was reprinted with an introduction by Woodstock Books in 1995, and an account of the man and his work has been written by Ian Fletcher: *Rediscovering Herbert Horne*, ELT Press, Greensboro, 1990.

First printed in *The Hobby Horse*, no.3, 1894.

Manuscript: In letter to Plarr of 17 January 1893.

Not remembering that he had withdrawn the poem from the *Second Book of the Rhymers' Club* (letter of c.15 October 1893, *Letters*, p.296), Dowson wrote to Plarr in April 1894 that 'They have chucked my Lady's Hands, and my Terre Promise, in favour of 2 verses which I like less' (*Letters*, p.305).

In a letter to George Arthur Greene about the submission to the Rhymers' Club book, the first line is mentioned with 'trailing' rather than 'drooping' in 'Even now, the fragrance of her drooping hair'. l.4 in the Plarr version is: 'Then what unsaid things trembled in the air!' As usual the corrections are in the interest of the languid mood and the elegant cadence.

p.99: **Autumnal**

Alexander Louis Teixeira de Mattos San Payo y Mendes (1865-1921) had a Dutch father and an English mother. He was a journalist who made a substantial reputation as a translator. He married Lily (née Sophie Lees), the widow of William Wilde, in 1900.

Manuscript: The three first stanzas are in a letter to Victor Plarr (*Letters*, pp.243-4), just after the death of Tennyson (6 October 1892), where it is called 'In Autumn' and the month in the first stanza given as September rather than October. The version in the letter to Plarr has some minor substitutions: 'move' for 'sway' in l.3; 'sunshine' for 'shadow' in l.8; and Dowson says that 'My muse awoke from her torpor of many months yesterday, here is her feeble utterance, but she may run to another verse by and by'. There is an unpublished letter in the Pierpont Morgan Library, MA.2524, where Dowson writes in French to A. Teixeira de Mattos at 3 Plowden Buildings in the Temple, recommending M. Lugné-Poe to 'Mon cher Ami', with the hope that his visit will remind Teixeira de Mattos that he has owed him a letter for six weeks and saying that Lugné-Poe 'a doré le souvenir de mon séjour à Pont-Aven'.

p.100: **In Tempore Senectutis**

Manuscript: In a letter to Victor Plarr of c. 26 October 1892 (*Letters*, pp.246-80, where it is dated '24/10/92', and has the epigraph '"Junior fui etenim senui" Ps. 37.25.' (i.e. I have been young and now am old). Dowson introduces it in the letter with the words: 'In the meanwhile a dyspeptic little poem, "to His Lady and His Friend"'.

p.101: **Villanelle of his Lady's Treasures**

First published in *Temple Bar*, August 1893.

p.102: **Gray Nights**

Charles Sayle (1864-1924) knew Lionel Johnson in his Winchester days and corresponded with him, figuring as 'Correspondent B' in *Some Winchester Letters of Lionel Johnson* (1919). He went up to New College Oxford where he was joined in 1886 by Johnson, who introduced him to Dowson. He graduated in 1887. Sayle was never a committed member of London homosexual society. He was briefly Librarian at Toynbee Hall, and went on to re-catalogue the library of St John's College, Cambridge, and then to join the staff of Cambridge University Library in 1893, becoming Assistant Librarian in 1910. His chief contribution to scholarship is in the *Catalogue of the Earlier English Books* in Cambridge University Library, but he also wrote four volumes of verse, including *Erotidia* (Rugby, 1889), and *Musa Consolatrix* (1893), which includes a sonnet to Ernest Dowson (reproduced as Appendix II in Desmond Flower's edition of *New Letters from Ernest Dowson*, Whittington Press, 1984). Sayle introduced Dowson to Plarr in 1888.

Manuscript: In a letter to John Gray, dated by Flower and Maas in February 1892 but perhaps later, there called 'To His Lady: A Nocturne'. Dowson, in sending it to Gray, comments that 'I wrote it last night after consuming many whiskeys, & it presumably contained then some intention in it. | This morning I found it, & it was absolutely unintelligible to me, & will remain so, I presume' (*Letters*, p.179). In l.2 the letter to Gray has 'tract' for 'track', which seems more appropriate, and we have followed that reading.

p.103: **Vesperal**

Hubert Montague Crackanthorpe (1870-1896) wrote decadent and naturalist short stories, published in collections of which the most notable are *Wreckage* (1893) and *Sentimental Studies* (1895). He had left Eton early to be tutored by Image, Gissing, and George Moore, and was in France between 1889 and 1892, meeting Mallarmé, Maeterlinck, the Goncourts and Gide. He edited the *Albemarle* in 1892, contributed to *The Yellow Book* and the *Savoy*, and was negotiating to succeed Symons as editor of the *Savoy* at the time of his death in 1896. The problems with his wife and mistress suggest that his drowning in the Seine was suicide. *Last Studies* (1897) was collected after his death, with an introduction by Henry James.

The italicised refrains are taken from Matthew, chapter 6, verse 34: 'Take therefore no thought for the morrow: for the morrow shall take thought for the things of itself. Sufficient unto the day is the evil thereof.'

p.104: **The Garden of Shadow**

First printed in the *Second Book of the Rhymers' Club* (1894), p.105.

p.105: *Soli cantare periti Arcades*

Aubrey Beardsley (1872-1898) burst onto the London art scene with his illustrations of *Le Morte Darthur* in 1893, and for the brief period of life that remained to him delighted and shocked the public with his revolutionary illustrations and designs. He was art editor of *The Yellow Book* and the *Savoy*, and among many other stunning designs, created the cover for Dowson's *Verses* and illustrations for *The Pierrot of the Minute*. Beardsley, like Dowson, was consumptive and destined not to live long, and their paths frequently crossed. Perhaps the reason why the supremely artificial Beardsley should be the dedicatee of this mock pastoral is exactly because it is a mock pastoral.

In Virgil's tenth Eclogue, he sings of the love of his friend C. Cornelius Gallus for a mistress who had deserted him. While Gallus was pining for an unrequited love, the shepherds came to comfort him.

> tristis at ille 'tamen cantabitis, Arcades' inquit,
> 'montibus haec vestris, soli cantare periti Arcades' (ll.31-2).

('But he sadly replied: "Yet you Arcadians will sing this tale to your mountains; Arcadians only know how to sing"'.)

p.107: **On the birth of a Friend's Child**

Victor Gustave Plarr and Helen (Nellie) Marion Plarr were friends of Dowson whom he met often for a period in the early nineties. Victor Plarr appears in Ezra Pound's *Hugh Selwyn Mauberley* as 'Monsieur Verog'. Plarr was born at Le Kupferhammer near Strasbourg on 21 June 1863, son of Dr Gustavus Plarr, a mathematician of Alsace, and an English mother, Mary Jane Tompkins. After the Franco-Prussian war, the Plarr family left Alsace for Scotland. Educated at Madras College, St. Andrews, at Tonbridge School, and Worcester College, Oxford, Plarr achieved a small degree of literary fame. In 1890 he became librarian of King's College, London and in 1897 librarian of the Royal College of Surgeons. He wrote the first book-length account of Dowson, entitled *Ernest Dowson 1888-1897: Reminiscences, Unpublished Letters and Marginalia* (Elkin Mathews, London, 1914). Plarr died on 28 January 1929. His *Collected Poems* were edited by Ian Fletcher in 1974 (Eric and Joan Stevens, London).

Manuscript: The poem is copied into a letter to Victor Plarr of c. 3 September 1893 (*Letters*, pp.290-291).

In a letter to Plarr of c.13 April 1894 (*Letters*, p.304), Dowson asks

Plarr to thank his mother 'for the symbolical stones according to the Polish tradition. I am intensely interested in every kind of that symbolism'.

The Plarrs' daughter Marion was born on 2 September 1893. She wrote the rather sensational novel based on the relationship between Dowson and Adelaide Foltinowicz, *Cynara: The Story of Ernest and Adelaide* (London, Grant Richards, 1933) which printed previously unseen correspondence between Dowson and Plarr, including the letter celebrating Marion's birth. This begins with the quotation from Horace's ode celebrating the safe return home of Numida (*Odes*, Book 1, Ode 36, line 10): 'Cressa ne careat alba Dies'. Dowson misremembers the exact line 'cressa ne careat pulchra dies nota', though he remembers the gist of it: 'let not the fair day want its mark of Cretan earth [i.e. chalk]', the central idea being that of a special day marked with white chalk. Indeed Dowson's formal couplets — what Dowson referred to as 'versicles pseudo 18th-cent.' — reflect the classical tone. The naming of Plarr as Eugenio suggests a well-born mortal whilst Egeria for Nellie Plarr refers to the Italian water-nymph to whom, in Roman religion, pregnant women were to make sacrifices in order to secure an easy delivery. (The first recorded use of the word 'eugenics' by the *OED* is in 1883 and Dowson's references to Eugenio may well have been inspired by the contemporary debate about eugenics, a dreary monument to which is Max Nordau's *Degeneration* (1895)). The letter also celebrates the acceptance by the Bodley Head of Plarr's book of poems *In the Dorian Mood*, which in the event was not published until 1896.

p.108: **Extreme Unction**

Lionel Johnson (1867-1902) was the diminutive, precocious and erudite scholar of the Rhymers' Club, to whom Yeats looked for authority. Yet he was tormented by his homosexuality, agonising over having introduced Wilde to Lord Alfred Douglas. He lived for a time in the Fitzroy Street house which was at the centre of much of the London literary world of the day, and knew many of the writers of the time. He wrote and reviewed widely, and published two important books of verse, *Poems* (1895) and *Ireland, with other poems* (1897) before declining into alcoholism. He shared Dowson's yearning for the 'measureless consummation' of Roman Catholicism, to which he was a convert in 1891. His poems have been edited by Ian Fletcher and reproductions of the original editions published by Woodstock Books in 1993 and 1996.

First printed in the *Second Book of the Rhymers' Club* (1894), p.6.

Manuscript: In a letter to Plarr of c. 28 November 1893 (*Letters*, pp.299-300).

Dowson wrote to Plarr, enclosing a copy of the poem, with the comment that 'Johnson to whom I have conveyed the weighty packet seems to like them the best of my budget' (*Letters*, p.299), which explains the dedication. Dowson is indebted to Flaubert's description of the administration of extreme unction in *Madame Bovary* (see Katherine Wheatley, *University of Texas Modern Language Notes*, 1923) and to the description at the very end of Pater's *Marius the Epicurean*: 'Gentle fingers had applied to hands and feet, to all those old passage-ways of the senses, through which the world had come and gone for him, now so dim and obstructed, a medicinable oil'. The version of l.1 in the Plarr letter is even closer to Pater: 'Upon the lips, the hands, the feet'. Dowson points out the resemblance of the passage in Pater to a passage in Zola's *Le Rêve* (1888) in a letter to Arthur Moore of January 1889, and goes on: You must read the "extreme unction" pages even if you can't stomach the whole. The purifying of the separate orifices of sensation with the consecrated oils strikes me as an excessively fine notion. I think if I have a death-bed (wh. I don't desire) I must be reconciled to Rome for the sake of that piece of ritual. It seems to me the most fitting exit for the epicurean — after all one is chiefly that — & one would procure it — (it seems essentially pagan) without undue compromise or affectation of a belief in "a sort of a something somewhere", simply as an exquisite sensation, & for the sensation's sake' (*Letters*, pp.21-2). Line 5 in the Plarr letter read: 'The roving feet that ran so fast'; and the 'Sacring oils' of l.13 had been 'healing Oils'.

p.109: **Amantium Irae**

Manuscripts: BM Add MS 45135, dated 15 March 1894, where it is called 'Here and Now'.

The title quotes Act III, scene iii, l.23 of Terence's *Andria*: 'Amantium irae amoris integratiost' ('Lovers' quarrels make their love stronger').

Dowson replaced 'shadow' with 'tempest' in l.4.

p.111: **Impenitentia Ultima**

Robert Harborough Sherard (1861-1943) is perhaps best remembered in this context as the man in whose house Dowson died in Catford in 1900. He was also friend and early biographer of Oscar Wilde and moved, like Dowson, between England and France.

First printed in the *Savoy*, no.1, January 1896.

Title: 'Final impenitence'.

Dowson, in a letter to John Gray of December 1895, invites Gray to look at his story in the *Savoy* and adds: ' also a poem, but that is rather pommade' (*Letters*, p.324). Dowson improves l.6 from the *Savoy*'s 'And that is why I must eat my bread in bitterness and sweat'.

p.112: **A Valediction**

Manuscripts: 1. On the back of a letter from a share-pusher, dated December 13, 1893 in the J. Harlin O'Connell Collection; 2. Written by Dowson in a copy of the *Second Book of the Rhymers' Club* (now [1946] in Michael Holland's Library) for Mr. de V. Payen Payne, who had asked Plarr and Dowson to write in his book; 3. BM Add MS 45135, dated 2 March 1894.

Dowson worked on the penultimate line; he tried 'And after harvest God's good time to sleep', 'And failing harvest' and 'Or if we reap not, a long time to sleep'.

p.113: **Sapientia Lunae**

André Lebey (1877-1938), French poet, whom Dowson would have met with the group round the *Mercure de France*, and with Davray, Lautrec, Louys.

Manuscripts: 1. Letter to Plarr of 3 March 1892; 2. Last stanza only on a loose leaf numbered 7 in the Flower notebook, on the reverse of the ms of 'After Paul Verlaine. Spleen', which is dated 'Feb 92'.

In explaining the wisdom of the moon to Henry Davray in a letter of June 1896, Dowson says that '"runes" were an ancient form of picture or symbol-writing used in Druidical times before writing was invented. As I use it, it means is little more than an archaic form of *oracle*. Mon idée peut être assez bien traduite par "oracles des roses"' (*Letters*, p.370). Davray was planning to publish a translation but it did not appear. The last two lines in Plarr's letter vary slightly:

> This said I, knowing all the rune of roses,
> Which in her hour the pale, soft moon discloses.

p.114: **'Cease smiling, Dear! a little while be sad'**

The epigraph is from Propertius, Book II, xii, 23: 'while the fates allow us, let us glut our eyes with love'.

p.116: **Seraphita**

See the note to 'Seraphita-Seraphitūs' above, p.218.

p.117: **Epigram**

Manuscript: A version of this neat reversal of the Pygmalion myth is located by Flower in the collection of C. Vincent Armstrong, entitled

'The Requital' and published in *Poetical Works* p.186. The last line has
the only significant variation:

Turn my live idol marble, and her heart – a stone!

p.118: *Quid non speremus, amantes?*

Arthur Collin Moore (1866-1952) shared Dowson's admiration for
Henry James and collaborated with him in two published novels, *A
Comedy of Masks* (1893) and *Adrian Rome* (1899) and other unpublished
novels. He met Dowson while a law student at Queen's College Oxford
and practised as a lawyer until 1937, while simultaneously attempting
to succeed as a writer of novels, of which he published several, and
stories, which he published in *Macmillan's Magazine* and *The Yellow Book*.
He is the most frequent recipient of Dowson's letters.

Manuscript: In a letter to Victor Plarr; dated '9/4/94' (*Letters*, pp.304-
5; Pierpont Morgan Library ms MA.2261).

The Latin title: 'What may we not hope for, o lovers?' comes from
Virgil's eighth Eclogue, l.26. Dowson quotes from the part of the poem
singing the despair of a jilted lover. The passage can be translated thus:
'Nysa is given to Mopsus. What can we lovers not look for? Griffins
will be mating with horses, and in time to come the timid deer will
come to drink with the dogs'. It is tempting to read Dowson's own
situation into this; perhaps Adelaide had indeed been given to another
as she approached her sixteenth birthday; and perhaps he thought her
future husband particularly unsuitable (our only description of him is
Jepson's account of 'a short, cylindrical German, with a large, round
head and a large, round, pale, shining face': *Memories of a Victorian*,
p.220). Dowson had proposed and been rejected the previous April,
and in the letter to Plarr which includes this poem he writes that 'the
first fortnight in April must be bound up with my fortunes very closely,
critically, or fatally, or perilously' (*Letters*, p.305).

p.119: **Chanson sans paroles**

In imitation, though not a translation, of Verlaine's *Romances sans
paroles* (1874).

Dowson frequently suggested that he was interested more in the
music of his poems than their meaning, as when he writes to Arthur
Moore that 'I have been writing verses, in the manner of the French
"symbolists": verses making for mere sound, and music, with just a
suggestion of sense, or hardly that; a vague Verlainesque emotion'
(*Letters*, p.190).

THE PIERROT OF THE MINUTE

The Pierrot of the Minute was published in 1897 by Leonard Smithers in an ordinary edition of three hundred copies with thirty copies of an edition de luxe on Japanese vellum. It was decorated with a frontispiece, initial letter, vignette and cul-de-lampe by Aubrey Beardsley. The small paper copies were bound in green cloth and the large paper copies in vellum; both editions were stamped in gold with a design by Beardsley on the front and back cover. Beardsey's original thought for the binding was: 'For the Dowson play cover I should suggest grey papered boards with a little white label on the back side'; but then he offered a design (*Letters of Aubrey Beardsley*, p.215). His comment in a letter to Smithers in February 1897: 'When does that foolish book *The Pierrot of the Minute* propose to be ready?' (*Ibid*, p.255) seems more a comment on the delay in publishing (he had finished the drawings in the previous November) than on the play. In March he wrote that 'The L.P. *Pierrot* is delightful' though it was probably the binding and his own designs he was thinking of. We tend to be of Malcolm Easton's opinion that Beardsley's reportedly harsh criticisms of Dowson seem 'to have been largely the invention of Vincent O'Sullivan' (*Aubrey and the Dying Lady*, p. 72).

Only 'The Moon Maiden's Song' had previously been published in the programme of the performance in the West Theatre of the Royal Albert Hall.

There are two manuscripts, both in the Lessing Rosenwald collection in the Library of Congress, the first page of one of which is reproduced in Mark Longaker's biography of Dowson and in his edition of the *Poems of Ernest Dowson* (1962). The two copies were from William Theodore Peters' collection and were those for the two actors in the piece, Peters himself and Miss Ida North. As one might expect from acting rather than reading texts, their major differences lie in the stage directions rather than the text, but a complete study must await a full edition of the play itself. We use the 1897 version, which Dowson had ample time to revise and correct, although others may have had a hand in preparing the piece for the press.

The play was commissioned in October 1892 by William Theodore Peters, an American actor-poet who was one of the 'permanent guests' at the Rhymers' Club. Given the time-scale, Dowson was characteristically impetuous in taking it on, and characteristically regretful at having done so; as he explained to Plarr in a letter of *c*.26 October 1892: 'Your letter should have been answered before this: but I have been frightfully busy, having rashly undertaken to make a little Pierrot play, in verse for Peters which is to be played at Aldershot, and afterwards at the Chelsea Town Hall: the article to be delivered in a fortnight. So until this period of severe mental agony be past, I can go nowhere' (*Letters*, p.246). Later in the letter he moans again: 'I would this play were done: half of it is completed and I have seven days more, but the second half is mightily oppressing me. And I am horribly afraid that when it is written I may be worried with rehearsals and enforced company with terrible South Kensington young ladies and fashionable Chelsea Mesdames'. He worked hard at it, discussing parts with Lionel Johnson and making some suggested emendations, but the limitations he had been set — not only of time — made it difficult. He wrote to Peters that he was afraid that 'with a limitation of two characters I can not attempt any dramatic effect. Is this required? Or will you be satisfied with a *folium rosae* which must depend entirely on its verses and the speaking of these to carry it through, with the help of the Pierrot's tradition? Would you by the way send me a line to say what you mean exactly with the extract of the fairy song you gave me?' (*Letters*, p.245). By the second of November he had finished it 'save only the song to your formula', and asked Peters to write an epilogue.

The performance at Aldershot was in fact postponed until 5 December, so that the first performance was at a concert for the Stanley Habitation of the Primrose League at Chelsea Town Hall at 8.15 in the evening of 22 November 1892. The Primrose League was a political association founded in 1883 in support of Lord Beaconsfield's style of conservatism, and the audience was 'very much confined to the actual Leaguites themselves', although Dowson reports that 'Gray, Teixeira, Horne, Symons and my people y seront' (*Letters*, p.254). Much to his dismay, Dowson was delegated by Peters and Mrs Hartshorne (obviously one of the Chelsea Mesdames he was dreading) to get from the Lord Chamberlain the licence for the play, which was in the event issued on the 16th. The event included music and songs, Dowson's 'Dramatic Fantasy', a presentation by Mr Hartshorne to Mr Whitmore M.P. on behalf of the Habitation, more songs and music and a comedietta called 'Man Proposes'. William Theodore Peters acted in Dowson's play opposite Miss Ida North, and 'The Moon Song' was composed by Mr Herbert Bunning and sung by Miss Scott. The two principals performed in it again in Aldershot on 5 December, and this time *The Lady* reported that 'The stringed band of the Royal Horse Artillery played 'The Moonlight Sonata' softly at intervals throughout'. It was performed in a private house, the 'studio of Miss Curtois, 5A Clareville Grove, Gloucester Rd. SW', on the 29 March, when Dowson had difficulty in drumming up his eight visitors (see *Letters*, pp.275-6). It was performed again in an afternoon concert in the West Theatre of the Royal Albert Hall on 4 May 1893, when Peters acted also in a 'Dramatic Vignette' called 'Une Marquise', adapted from Austin Dobson. The 'Vignette' was followed by a concert of songs and music, followed by Dowson's 'Dramatic Phantasy', with incidental music by Noel Johnson and the Moon Maidens' Song sung by Miss Alice Davies. The last performance which Dowson mentions in his letters is in July 1893, when Dowson asks Peters to send a ticket to John Lane. Plarr's footnote (*Ernest Dowson . . . Reminiscences . . .*, p.66) that Mabel Beardsley was in the Albert Hall Theatre performance is not borne out by the programme, and the fact that Beardsley does not mention her in all the correspondence when he writes about the play suggests that Plarr misremembered.

Peters's style and appearance can be judged from Dowson's description to Moore in his letter of 22 November 1892. They had seen Jane May as Pierrot in *L'Enfant prodigue* in 1891 and Dowson says that Peters's 'Pierrot looks more perfect even than Jane, and more like a girl. He has borrowed a superb buckle from Lady Mount Temple, part of the Palmerston diamonds; and looks dazzling. He acts well too, though in a big Hall, I fear he may be rather overheard than heard' (*Letters*, p.254).

Dowson was not indifferent to the fate of his play. He made sure that his friends saw it and twice sent Lane invitations. His father seems to have been energetic in its promotion, writing to Peters suggesting that he send a ticket for the Aldershot production to the *Dramatic and Sporting News*, who would probably give him a notice and perhaps even a sketch (letter of 2 December 1892 in the Berg Collection). And Dowson made serious attempts to arouse professional interest in it as a curtain-raiser or a piece for soirées. He sent it to Oscar Wilde in March 1893, perhaps for him to consider it as a curtain-raiser for *A Woman of No Importance*, which was to be opened at the Haymarket in April; and he reported that 'Another person has written to me about it from the Lyceum a stranger to me (Miss Vanburgh) and I have been obliged to defer sending it to her until I hear the Haymarket decision' (*Letters*, p.273).

He reports to Peters in May 1893 that he has sent a copy to the actor Courtenay Thorpe (1854-1927) (*Letters*, p.280). And he tells Arthur Moore in September 1893 that 'I have had another enquiry anent my play: this time from the provinces, viâ the "Professional World"' (*Letters*, p.291).

When the play was included in Symons's edition of the poems, it reached a wider audience, and it became even better known when it was used to supply the libretto for Granville Bantock's 'Comedy Overture' (1908), which Plarr went to hear in the Queen's Hall in December 1913.

LA PUCELLE, VARIANTS OF CANTOS XVII AND XXI

Dowson's translation of Voltaire's *La Pucelle: The Maid of Orleans* was published in two volumes in 1899, in a limited edition of 500 copies, for the Lutetian Society. The Lutetian Society was in effect a front for the publication of advanced and risqué literature, designed to avoid the danger of being imprisoned, as Henry Vizetelly had recently been, for publishing translations of Zola. Dowson's translation of *La Terre* (1894) had been published under its imprint. The covers were plain white with quarter binding in blue, with gold lettering on the spine only.

Jeroom Vercruysse, the editor of the *La Pucelle* volume of the standard edition of Voltaire (general editor Theodore Besterman), opens his introduction by describing the poem as Voltaire's most derided and least read work. Though enormously popular in its day, its suspect reputation in subsequent years was more often than not based on little or no knowledge of the text, on prejudice, or on misapprehension frequently derived from the numerous pirated and corrupted editions which were available.

Voltaire's poem in its complete form was a work of over eight and a half thousand lines in twenty one Cantos (or twenty two if we include the 'Corisandre' variant). It was the work of thirty or so years, from about 1730 onwards when Voltaire was in his mid thirties. Its long gestation accounts in great part for its variety and apparent lack of homogeneity. It grew in size and popularity as it amused the number of his friends and a curious public, and leaked out into pirated editions until Voltaire finally published an authorised text in 1762. Nancy Mitford in *Voltaire in Love* (London, 1957, p.70) described it as 'one of the most unseemly poems, according to Lord Morley, that exist in any tongue. Of all Voltaire's works *La Pucelle* was his own most cherished darling; for years he went on adding to it and polishing it up'. The poem was, according to Vercruysse, almost known by heart by a whole generation, but its reputation, at home and abroad, suffered severely from prudes and the censorious. When Lady Charleville published her translation into English in 1796-97, it is reported that the family tried to gather back (presumably for destruction) the fifty or so copies that were produced. In 1892, F. Espinasse in his *Life of Voltaire* (London, 1892, p.77) called the book 'the most disgraceful of all Voltaire's writings', while J. Morley in his *Voltaire* (London, 1893, p.147) said that it had 'at least the wit of a rational man, and not the prying beastliness of a satyr' (quoted in Vercruysse, p.213). This was the book which Leonard Smithers, realising that it was on that boundary between the scholarly and the almost pornographic which he trod so astutely, asked Dowson to translate in 1895.

The poem had retained its interest if only as one of Voltaire's works, and over ninety editions had been published before Dowson came to translate it. The most recent edition available to him in 1895 was a reprint of the Garnier edition of 1881, itself a re-impression of the Beuchot edition of 1833. Such editions printed the poem in twenty-one cantos with extensive variants in appendices.

Dowson began his work in 1895 and originally agreed to translate it from scratch, but this proved too onerous a task. In a letter to Arthur Moore of 22 and 27 December 1895 (*Letters*, p.334-6) he wrote that 'Instead of translating the Pucelle as originally arranged I am merely revising an old English translation.' In fact he made use of *two* translations, those which he announces on the title page: that of Lady Charleville and that of W. H. Ireland published in 1822. There had been two translations into English before these (in 1758 and 1785-86), but only of the earlier cantos. Lady Charleville's, Ireland's and Dowson's are the only three translations into English of the whole twenty one Cantos which make up the standard edition, and Dowson's is the only one to attempt the variants.

The poem, a light-hearted burlesque, which nonetheless treats some serious subjects on its way, has as its central theme gentle ridicule of the idea that the power of France depended on sustaining the virginity of Joan of Arc. It is perhaps inevitable that such a topic, and a defence of her virginity over twenty-one cantos, would include some ribald scenes which might be shocking to the conventional. But Dowson, who in 1891 wished his own character to include "a little dash of Voltaire", might well have defended Voltaire's *La Pucelle* as he defended the work of Sir Richard Burton in his diatribe "Against My Lady Burton".

The title page of Dowson's *La Pucelle* declares that it is 'A new and complete translation into English verse revised corrected and augmented from the earlier English translation of W. H. Ireland and the one attributed to Lady Charleville with the variants now for the first time translated into English by Ernest Dowson'. That description is exactly right. He uses both his source translations and corrects and adds to them when he feels that their rendering of the French is either inadequate or inelegant. He is not, of course, consistent: there are times when he depends more heavily on Ireland but there are equally times when he depends heavily on Lady Charleville, and times when he feels that he needs to be independent of them both. To read through the Dowson text with the French text, the Lady Charleville text and the Ireland text spread out in front of one is to find a new respect for Dowson's care and industry. That he took his job seriously and did not simply reproduce either Ireland or Lady Charleville explains why it took him so long and why he would write of his pains with the task. On c.22 March 1896 he wrote to John Gray that he was 'editing the most tedious & uncongenial work which I have read' (*Letters*, p.349). He reported to Smithers in April that he was 'getting on, though slowly' (p.353) and was calling it the 'interminable "Pucelle"' a fortnight later. Flower and Maas suggest that as late as May 1897 he is still revising it (*Letters*, p.383).

The following brief example, selected somewhat at random, may serve to suggest the sort of thing that happens throughout the length of the twenty one books, and to show how Dowson was not simply plagiarising, and why it took him such a time. We will give the French original followed by the versions by Ireland, Lady Charleville and finally by Dowson. Here is the text of Canto VIII lines 26-32, as printed in the standard text: Jeroom Vercruysse, ed., *La Pucelle d'Orléans, Edition critique*, volume 7 of *The Complete Works of Voltaire*, Institut et Musée Voltaire, Les Delices, Geneva, 1970, p.392:

De Jeanne d'Arc cependant, cher lecteur,
En ce moment je ne puis rendre compte.
Car Dorothée et Dunois son vengeur,
Et la Trimouille objet de son ardeur,
Ont de grands droits, a j'avoûrai sans honte
Qu'avec raison vous vouliez être instruit
Des beaux effets que leur amour produit.

Here is Ireland's Translation:

Still nought can I my friend, of Joan here sing,
Since now the muse of Dorothy takes wing,
And Dunois, the avenging champion brave,
And Trimouille well-beloved, her faithful slave,
Each having on my verse the rightful claim;
And I must here confess, devoid of shame,
That with just cause, my reader now enquires
What feats were kindled by these Paphian fires.

Here is Lady Charleville's version:

But yet, dear Reader, 'tis not in my pow'r,
To occupy with Joan the present Hour.
Since brave Dunois and Dorothea fair,
And tender La Tremouille demand my care.
Nor shall I blush to tell whilst you approve
The tender sequel of their constant Love.

And here is Dowson's version:

But yet, dear Reader, 'tis not in my power,
To occupy with Joan the present hour;
Since Dorothy, Dunois, her champion,
And La Tremouille who all her love had won,
Each have upon my verse a rightful claim;
And I must here confess, devoid of shame,
That with just cause, the reader may enquire
What was the sequel of their tender fire.

Dowson takes his first two lines from Lady Charleville. He rejects both versions for the next two lines, but creates a new rhyme by using Ireland's rendering of 'vengeur' while refusing his introduction of 'slave' as unauthorised; he then switches to Ireland's version for the next two lines and a half but searches in his last line and a half for a plainer version than either, although using words suggested by one or the other.

Dowson does the same sort of thing throughout the twenty-one Cantos. He takes one of the texts whenever the translation is plain and flowing, changes to the other if the phrasing gets awkward or stilted, modifies one or the other version slightly or translates for himself when neither is satisfactory. I have not gone through the whole two volumes with this care, but the impression received by checking a hundred lines or so of each canto indicated that the same process is going on throughout. Dowson is happy to depend on his models when they are doing a good job, but he moves between them or abandons them whenever they strike him as inadequate. It is not a lazy piece of work.

There are translations of the variants throughout the text. Many variants, both genuine and spurious, were published in the editions of Voltaire which were printed in the eighteenth and nineteenth centuries, and these variants range from a phrase up to whole cantos. They do not appear in Charleville or Ireland but Dowson assiduously translates a good number and gives them as footnotes to his text.

To publish the whole translation would rather overweight this present book with material which was neither Dowson's original work nor even his translation. To publish the variants only (which *are* his translation) would be rather fragmentary and not give the pieces a context which would help them to make sense. However, it did seem worth taking account of the two occasions where Dowson translates whole Cantos, so that we can see his ability to handle story, rhyme and language with a certain grace, however much the content might verge on pornography.

We therefore reprint two variants from *La Pucelle* which constitute whole Cantos: the variants to Cantos XVII and XXI. They are different in origin. The variant of Canto XVII, called 'Corisandre', is thought to be Voltaire's, unlike most of the published variants. It is numbered XIV.a. in Volume 7 of the *Complete Works*. It first appeared in the pirated London printing of 1756 and became established as part of the text in all editions after 1785. Although there are no allusions to it by Voltaire nor are there any authoritative manuscripts, its relationship to Canto XVII and the fact that two passages are used elsewhere, suggest it was simply superseded (see the relationship between the opening twenty or so lines and the opening of Canto XXI). The variant of Canto XXI is however unlikely to be Voltaire's, first appearing in pirated editions of 1755 and 1756.

The reader is referred to the *Complete Works* for annotation and further detail about the complex and convoluted story of the whole text.

DECORATIONS

Decorations was published by Leonard Smithers in December 1899. There is no record of the size of the edition, but it is likely to have been almost as limited as that of *Verses*. The binding, of white vellum, has a design by Althea Gyles stamped in gold, featuring a rose on the front cover and on the back cover a quadrant of rose stems behind which a winged arm holds one of the stems. It is signed with a monogram in the corner. The book was printed by the Chiswick Press.

Dowson corrected the proofs in the summer of 1899 and sent them back to Smithers with an apology that he would have sent more of his translation of Goncourt 'only the poems what with arranging and *redigeant* have taken up all my time' (*Letters*, p.414).The proofs are now in the Berg Collection in New York Public Library. The copy is dated by the printer three times in the text on pp.[1], 17 and 33: '31 8 99'. There are a small number of minor corrections, which will be mentioned under the individual poems, but the major change involves the title and the title page. Dowson had been uncertain about a title. He wrote to Smithers when he returned the proofs that 'the title I have used is quite discretional. I can think of nothing better' (*Letters*, p.414). When he soon afterwards sent some further verses and the prose poems, he added that 'Your title "Poems in Prose and Verse" — seems all right. That I suggested was in despair of a good inclusive title' (*Letters*, p.415). Certainly the original title on the proof, 'Love's Aftermath' would apply only to part of the collection. The proof title page also included the four lines from Propertius, which he had copied out on the title page of his 'Paris fragments' notebook in 1897 (see p.6 above) to indicate again his dedication to Adelaide. They correspond to the preface in his first volume of poems, and are addressed to Cynthia in a mood of fear that she might love another: 'You alone are my home, Cynthia, you alone are my parents, you are my every moment of happiness. Whether I am downcast or joyful when I meet my friends, I shall say "Cynthia was the cause"'. The proof copy lacks the final two pages (49-50) on which the book prints 'The Princess of Dreams', as if this disillusioned farewell was a last addition to his text.

IN VERSE

p.173: **Beyond**

First printed in *Temple Bar*, September 1893.

Manuscript: 1. Flower notebook, p.51, dated 'Aug. 1889' and annotated in pencil 'Temple Bar'; annotated on facing page: 'Published. / Sept. 1893 Temple Bar'; 2. Longaker in *The Poems of Ernest Dowson*, reproduces another manuscript version (p.214), then in the possession of C Warren Force, now in the collection of Mark Samuels Lasner.

This poem, set as an epigraph for the whole book before the division into verse and prose, uses as its refrain the words which were set up as the original title of the book: 'Love's Aftermath'.

Dowson did not seem settled on his title: in the Flower notebook it is called 'To Hélène – A Rondeau' and in *Temple Bar* it is called 'A Roundel'. He sent a copy to Moore on 22 August 1889 and reported in a subsequent letter that *Temple Bar* had taken it, so that he could look forward to a welcome guinea (*Letters*, pp.101 and 106-7). They took three years to publish.

Dowson's corrections remove the medievalising tone: 'ywis' in l.1 becomes 'I think', 'erstwhile' or 'erewhile' become 'yesterday' in l.5. Lines 9-10 originally read: 'Thy lips are cold; Thy saddened eyes avow / Our short sweet love is done, we can but part'. This change allowed him to use without repetition 'saddest' for 'bitterest' in l.3.

p.175: **De Amore**

Manuscripts: On three leaves slipped into the Flower notebook from another notebook and numbered 12 to 14..

Title 'Of love'. The placing of love as the supreme god threatens the place of Christ, which is emphasised in the deleted conclusion:

> Foiled, frustrate and alone, and crucified,
> > Go with me all my way
> > And let me not blaspheme.

Dowson had problems with the conclusion, completing up to l.46 in one ink, then adding two lines, and then a further four in another ink and hand. In proof, the provisional title for the book, 'Love's Aftermath', had been printed above 'De Amore'.

p.177: **The Dead Child**

First printed in *Atalanta*, February 1893.

The *Atalanta* version changes detail but not tone. Lines 6-10 for example, read:

> Thy little life
> Was mine a little while;
> No fears were rife,
> To trouble the brief smile
> With stress or strife.

Lines 29--30 read:

> I too would come thy way,
> And, somewhere, rest.

The poem is related in its first line and in other aspects of its subject and construction to the much earlier poem 'After Many Years' (p.31), which Dowson never published.

p.179: **Carthusians**

Manuscripts: 1. Flower notebook, pp.77-78, dated '27 / May 91'; 2. BM Add MS 45135 with same date.

Dowson reports in a lettter to Arthur Moore of 3 April 1891 that 'I spent Monday at a Carthusian monastery in Sussex: Cowfold. An adorable place, high up and away from everywhere. Beata Solitudo! Perpetual silence! It is an enchanting order: they scarcely live in community, having separate cells in which they live, eat, read & meditate: once a week, for an hour, they may mix with each other & converse. For the rest they see each other only at the various offices: and pass each other in the cloister with a formal bow and a "memento mortis, frater!" Enchanting people! I hear that it is possible to go down and stay with them for two or three days: I shall try and work it' (*Letters*, p.191). Dowson refers to these verses as 'a pendant to the "Ursulines" [i.e. "Nuns of the Perpetual Adoration"]' in a letter to Moore of 29 May 1891 (*Letters*, p.201).

Line 6 is an excellent example of Dowson's small alterations for great improvement of the tune. It had originally read 'Only a sacred silence, as of death obtains'.

In the Flower notebook the final two stanzas seem a later coda after a conclusion reminiscent of the end of 'Nuns of the Perpetual

Adoration'. Line 32 caused problems: first it read 'None whispers that the shadow of death is on his heart', which was corrected to 'Who dares to say that Death's hard hand is on his heart'. The penultimate line of the poem originally read: 'Possess your visions still, possess the aching Christ'.

p.181: **The Three Witches**

First printed in The *Savoy*, no.6, October 1896, p.75.

Astarte was the Semitic goddess of fecundity, identified with the moon, worshipped in sacred groves, denounced in the Old Testament. Her cult in later times was combined with orgiastic celebration.

p.182: **Villanelle of the Poet's Road**

Dowson has noted on the proofs, where it was set straight through without breaks, that it should be printed in stanzas of three lines, with a final stanza of four lines.

Dowson is not the originator of the phrase 'wine and woman and song'. In 1862 Thackeray, translating lines attributed to Luther, wrote in *The adventures of Philip*: 'As Dr Luther sang, Who loves not wine, woman, and song, He is a fool his whole life long'. Luther seems to have added song to an older association of wine and women.

p.183: **Villanelle of Acheron**

Ms in Flower notebook, p.59, dated '25/3/90'. There is a note on the page which now faces this poem, which says 'Accepted "Atalanta" Oct 1890', but the poem did not appear there, and the note almost certainly refers to 'The Dead Child' on the missing page, which did.

Dowson corrected the proof to introduce the stanza breaks of the conventional villanelle, as with the previous poem. His original draft of l.8 was typically medieval: 'Ywis at last 'tis well to be' and l.14 was 'In sleep that wakes not easily'.

In Greek mythology Acheron is one of the five rivers surrounding Hades, the river Milton describes as 'sad Acheron, of sorrow dark and deep', which the souls of the dead had to bathe in or cross.

p.184: **Saint Germain-en-Laye**

First printed in the *Savoy*, no.II, April 1896, p.55.

Manuscript: In a letter to John Gray of 27 December 1895, in which Dowson writes that 'I adjoin my latest — which was chiefly written at the place whence I first wrote to you' (*Letters*, p.337). Dowson's previous letter to Gray in the same month had been written on paper of the Hôtel Colbert, Saint Germain-en-Laye.

The version in the letter to Gray had 'barren' for 'sullen' in l.3, 'ruddy' for 'roseal' in l.14, and the penultimate line read: 'Have tossed and torn, through all the barren years'.

St. Germain is a Paris suburb which Dowson visited in 1895, where he hoped to stay in 1896 and where he wished to stay in 1899. The dates after the title presumably refer to a memory of an earlier visit.

p.185: **After Paul Verlaine, I**

Manuscripts: 1. Flower notebook, p.80, dated 'Sept. 8th. 1891'; 2. In a letter to Arthur Moore (*Letters*, p.215) dated 8 September 1891 and now in the Berg collection of the New York Public Library.

Dowson always admired Verlaine, from whom he probably took the habit of dedicating individual poems to friends. He compared himself to Verlaine in a letter of 5 July 1896, when he wrote to Symons that 'I have always had, alas! Too much of that "swift, disastrous & suicidal energy" which destroyed our dear & incomparable Verlaine' (*Letters*, pp.371-372). Dowson met Verlaine at a lecture at Barnard's Inn in High Holborn in November 1893, and subsequently went to dinner, and they met again barely a month before Verlaine's death in 1896. This poem translates a poem from Verlaine's *Romances sans paroles* (1874), which also lacks a title save for the quotation from Rimbaud, simply recording that 'It rains gently on the town', which was presumably the stimulus for Verlaine's poem. Dowson adhered closely to the metre as well as the sense of his source.

The version in the letter to Moore changes the archaic 'mine' and 'hath' to 'my' and 'has', and gives 'sound' of the rain instead of 'fall' in line 5. Dowson introduces it to Moore as 'an attempt to translate a thing of Verlaine: Of course it is a failure' (*Letters*, pp.215-216).

p.186: **After Paul Verlaine, II, Colloque Sentimental**

There is a manuscript on a separate sheet in the Pierpont Morgan Library, MA.1952. A version of this poem was presumably on the missing p.81 of the Flower notebook, since an alternative to l.15 is written on p.80v: 'So through the madding oats they wandered', attempting to represent Verlaine's 'Tels ils marchaient dans les avoines folles'.

This is a translation of a poem with the same name from Verlaine's *Fêtes Galantes* (1869). Dowson has adhered to the metre as well as the sense of his original.

p.187: **After Paul Verlaine, III, Spleen**

Manuscripts: Loose leaf 8a in Flower notebook, dated 'Feb. 1892'.

This poem is a translation from Verlaine's *Romances sans paroles* (1874). Dowson has adhered closely to the metre of his original. John Gray included a translation of the same poem in *Silverpoints* (1893).

p.188: **After Paul Verlaine, IV**

Verlaine's original is in *Sagesse* (1881).

p.189: **To His Mistress**

Manuscript: Flower notebook pp.55-6 with pencilled note opposite: '*Rejected — Longmans — / Universal Review'.

Line 4 originally read 'Has terminus in time' and l.7 read 'eternal' for 'immortal'.

p.190: **Jadis**

Manuscripts: Flower notebook, p.53, where it is called 'Rondeau' and dated August 24th/89.

Dowson translates the title with his first word, in this form of rondeau which he tended to use. Line 6 in the notebook read: 'Your head the sunshine tinged with gold'.

p.191: **In a Breton Cemetery**

First printed in *The Pageant* 1897, p.232.

Manuscripts: 1. In a letter to John Gray with the addition of 'Pont Aven | March/96' (*Letters*, p.350) in Manchester University Library; 2. In the British Library, Add. MS 45135, dated as in the *Pageant* 'Pont-Aven, Finistère, 1896'; 3. On the fly -leaf of a book in the collection of Michael Holland, written at Pont-Aven in August 1896.

Dowson describes this to Gray as a 'versicle du pays'. The *Pageant* version was called 'On a Breton Cemetery'; offered 'stormy' for 'anxious' days in l.2, 'passion-tossed' for 'tempest-tost' in l.14, 'sleepy' for 'quiet' in l.16 and 'wan' for 'pale' in l.17. Lines 11-12 seemed most difficult to settle, with variants of 'Dimly, interminably [or 'mechanically'] / The same poor [or 'sad'] rosary'.

p.192: **To William Theodore Peters on his Renaissance Cloak**

William Theodore Peters (1862-1904) was an American-born actor and poet who commissioned Dowson to write *The Pierrot of the Minute* for which he was producer and leading actor in 1892 and 1893. He also seems to have commissioned these verses on his Italian cloak. Dowson wrote in early July 1893 to ask 'What are the precise embroideries on your cherry coloured cloak — fruit or flowers?' (*Letters*, p.281), and he supplied the verses with the modest disclaimer: 'I am glad you like the Versicles: I wish they were more worthy of you' (*Letters*, p.283). Peters apparently had some suggested amendments and Dowson wrote again in early August: 'Herewith, my dear Peters, the dedicatory verses as amended. I like "silk and silver" better than "green etc" — but as you will notice I have suggested the apple leaves in verse one. Do you think that so, it will do?' The 'silk and silver' duly appear in stanza 2 but there is no sign of the apple leaves. Dowson also wondered whether the poem would 'commend itself to Gleeson White'; he was perhaps hoping to pubish it in the *Studio*.

Peters was a close fried of Dowson for the early years of the 1890s, and was a 'permanent guest' at the Rhymers' Club. His *Posies out of Rings and Other Conceits* was published in 1896 and contains his epilogue to Dowson's playlet. Shortly after appearing in Dowson's play, he himself wrote *The Tournament of Love* (Paris, 1894), a pastoral masque in one act. He died in poverty in Paris.

p.193: **The Sea-change**

Manuscript: In a manuscript in the Morgan Library as 'Sea-Dreams'.

'Point du Pouldu' was added to the proofs. Le Poldu is situated south of Pont Aven in Brittany where Dowson spent much of 1896. There are verbal parallels with Swinburne's 'The Triumph of Time' from *Poems and Ballads: First Series* (1866). In the manuscript version of 'Amor Umbratilis' Dowson quotes the following lines from 'The Triumph of Time':

'*Umbratilis* - retiring; cf.

> I will keep my soul in a place out of sight
> Far off, where the pulse of it is not heard.'

The title in the Flower notebook was 'Sea-Dreams' and the poem was dated '1896 Point du Poldu'. There were some variations, most significantly in the reversal of stanzas two and three. Line 4 originally began with 'I will take my bark'; 'the mad winds are unreined' of l.7 replace 'the wild winds are unchained'; the present l.13 was originally 'I ~~will~~ shall be thine, my Sea! At last, thy kisses on my face'; l.15 began: 'Shall pass as the dreams and days have past'; and 'know' of the penultimate line was in the past tense.

p.194: **Dregs**

The alternative title, corrected in proof, was 'Vale'.

Dowson obviously remembered Swinburne's 'A Ballad of Burdens' with its line: 'This is the end of every man's desire'. He perhaps also remembered Robert Bridges's 'Elegy on a Lady, whom Grief for the death of her Betrothed Killed', which has the lines:

And thou, O lover, that art on the watch,
Where, on the banks of the forgetful streams,
The pale indifferent ghosts wander, and snatch
The sweetest moments of their broken dreams ....
But the music is still his own.

p.195: **A Song**

First printed in the *Savoy*, no.5, September 1896, p.36.
The French 'ma mie' is an affectionate 'my sweet, my love'.

p.196: **Breton Afternoon**

First published in the *Savoy*, No 3, July 1896, p40.
Line 9 had 'World' for 'land' and 'dark' for 'deep' in l.12. The last two lines were changed to italic at proof stage.

It seems likely that Dowson is referring to this poem 'in my Breton manner' in a letter to Leonard Smithers of early April 1896, which reports he is also working on his translation of Voltaire's *La Pucelle* and his story — probably 'The Dying of Francis Donne' (*Letters*, p.353).

p.197: **Venite Descendamus**

First published in the *Savoy*, No 4, August 1896, p.41.
The only potential source we have found for the Latin title ('come let us go down') is in Genesis 11, 7: 'Venite igitur descendamus et confundamus ibi linguam eorum ut non audiat unus quisque vocem proximi sui' ('Therefore let us go down and mix up their language, so that they may not be able to understand one another'). There is little to relate this passage about the Tower of Babel to Dowson's poem, however, except the vanity of words.

p.198: **Transition**

Manuscripts: Flower notebook, p.68, where it is dated 'Dec 26 '90'.
Line 14 in the notebook read 'The ~~slow decay~~ sadder things of autumn'. The last line seems to have caused most problem; Dowson tried 'While from the wintry sky there shines no sun', 'Beneath the dim receding[?] of the sun', 'Beneath their paler [?] whiteness [?] the wan sun' and 'The sky is desolate; there is no sun' before offering the printed line, which demands the 1890s pronunciation of 'decadence' with the stress on the second syllable.

p.199: **Exchanges**

p.200: **To a Lady Asking Foolish Questions**

There is a manuscript of the last two lines on a loose page in the Flower notebook which merely differ in having no punctuation.

p.201: **Rondeau**

p.202: **Moritura**

First printed in *London Society*, March 1887.

Dowson had used the word 'morituri' in the epigraph of his 'Sonnet to Nature' (see p.42), where he quotes Suetonius' salutation of the gladiators. Here those about to die are far less heroic, and more in keeping with Dowson's twilight tone, established very early in this poem, written and published before he was twenty.

p.203: **Libera Me**

Manuscript: Flower notebook, pp.3-4, where it is called 'Hymn to Aphrodite'. It was only the second poem transcribed into his notebook.

The plea to 'deliver me' in this very early, Swinburnian poem is addressed to Aphrodite, the goddess of love and beauty, who is known as the Cyprian because of her association with Paphos on Cyprus, the most ancient seat of her worship. Dowson would be familiar with the phrase 'libera me' in various parts of Catholic liturgy. A glance through the Roman Missal reveals it for example in the Tract for Good Friday, in the Tract for Palm Sunday, in the Gradual for the Sunday within the Octave of Corpus Christi and in the Introit for the 9th Sunday after Pentecost. It also occurs in Psalms 7, 22 and 140.

p.204: **To a Lost Love**

p.205: **Wisdom**

Manuscript: The Flower notebook, p.47v and 49, where the original title was 'This is the Wisdom of the wise'. This is probably the nearest we get to seeing Dowson working out rather than correcting a poem.

The manuscript version reads:

> Love wine and beauty and the spring
> ~~Though~~ While
> ~~The while the~~ wine is red ~~and love~~ & spring is here
> ~~Is not to tired~~
> And through the almond blossoms ring
> The dove-like voices of thy dear.

> Love wine and spring and beauty ~~while till~~ while
> Thy dear love
> ~~The wine grows pale and~~
> ~~The~~ The wine hath flavour and spring masks
> ~~And~~ Her ~~flaunting beauty in a smile~~

Her treachery in so soft a smile
~~That who shall dream of toil & tasks~~
That none may think of toil and tasks.

Dream all thy dreams and dream them well, ~~true~~
But when spring goes on hurrying feet
Look not thy sorrow in the eyes,
Consume ~~But take~~ the bitter with the sweet
This is the wisdom of the wise.

There even seems to be a tentative start on a new stanza with 'When'
and 'Love Laurel' crossed out.

p.206: In Spring

A dedication to Charles Conder was deleted after the proof stage.
Conder (1868-1909), an English-born painter with formative experience
in Australia, was a convivial companion of Dowson and Wilde after
Wilde's release. Dowson reported Wilde describing his conversation
as 'like a beautiful sea-mist'. Conder's elegant fans and paintings on
silk are a charming emblem of the 1890s.

Manuscripts: Flower notebook p.29-30, where it is called 'A Song for
Spring Time'.

There are minor adjustments to the first stanza — 'green bedecked'
replaces 'decked in green' and l.7 began 'It cometh' — but the opening
of the second stanza was the most altered. The original draft had:

The sleepy song of the
~~Mingles the murmur of~~ early bees
~~With rustling leaves in the budding trees~~
The jonquil flaunteth her yellow head

with the final version of l.9 suggested on the opposite page.

p.207: A Last Word

First printed in the *Savoy*, no.7, November 1896, p.87.

Manuscripts: Flower notebook, p.17, sonnet viii, the Epilogue, of the
sequence 'Sonnets of a Little Girl'. See pp.25 and 207 for the original
poem and the note on its development. Though the basic shape of the
poem was set out early before Dowson was twenty, the final corrections
probably date from the time when he was preparing it for the *Savoy*
and indicate how far he had come in strength and musicality.

IN PROSE

Dowson rarely mentions his prose poems. He does so in a letter to Smithers when he is sending off copy of his poems (dated June 1899 in *Letters*, p.414): 'The prose poems I will send on. But do you think they will go well together?' He thought that Smithers' proposed title 'Poems in Prose and Verse' was 'all right' (*Letters*, p.415), obviously adding the 'Decorations' at a late stage.

p.209: The Fortunate Islands

The Fortunate Islands were supposed by the ancient Greeks and Romans to be the place where the souls of the virtuous would go after death, and lay west of the Pillars of Hercules in the Atlantic. They are often identified with the Canaries.

p.210: Markets, after an Old Nursery Rhyme

The old nursery rhyme in question is presumably 'Where are you going to, my pretty maid?' with its assertion that the maiden's face is her fortune, she herself the object for sale.

p.211: Absinthia Taetra

The adjective describing absinthe means 'hateful, abominable, loathsome'. 'Opaline' is either a variety of chalcedony that has an opalescent quality, or a semi-transparent glass, whose other name of 'milk-glass' suggests Dowson's meaning. Absinthe becomes milky with the addition of water.

p.212: The Visit

p.213: The Princess of Dreams

The pages on which this prose poem appears are not in the proof in the Berg Collection.

Like 'Markets', this prose poem views dreams as pure fancy and sees the grubby reality of things. Coming as it does at the end of the book, it balances the 'Preface: for Adelaide' at the beginning of *Verses*, and, since there were no proof pages, one imagines it was a last-minute addition which constitutes a final recognition that Dowson's idealistic image of Adelaide has been a delusion.

SELECT BIBLIOGRAPHY

Primary Works (listed chronologically)

A Comedy of Masks, a novel, with Arthur Moore, 3 vols, Heinemann, 1893
La Terre by Emile Zola, translated for the Lutetian Society, 1894.
Majesty by Louis Couperus, translated with A. Teixeira de Mattos, T. Fisher Unwin, 1894.
Dilemmas: Stories and Studies in Sentiment, Mathews, 1895.
The History of Modern Painting by Richard Muther, translated with G. A. Greene and A. C. Hillier, 3 vols, Henry & Co, 1895-6.
La fille aux yeux d'or by Honoré de Balzac, Smithers, 1896.
Verses, Smithers, 1896.
The Pierrot of the Minute, a dramatic phantasy in one act, Smithers, 1897.
Les liaisons dangeureuses by Choderlos de Laclos, 2 vols, privately printed, 1898.
Adrian Rome, a novel, with Arthur Moore, Methuen, 1899.
La Pucelle by Voltaire, verse translation for the Lutetian Society, 1899.
Memoirs of Cardinal Dubois by Paul Lacroix, 2 vols, Smithers, 1899.
Decorations: in Verse and Prose, Smithers, 1899.
The Poems of Ernest Dowson, ed. T. B. Mosher, Portland, Maine, 1902.
The Poems of Ernest Dowson with a memoir by Arthur Symons, Lane, 1905.
Cynara, a little book of verse, T. B. Mosher, Portland, Maine, 1907.
The Confidantes of a King. The Mistresses of Louis XV by Edmond and Jules de Goncourt, 2 vols, T. N. Foulis, Edinburgh, 1907.
Poems and Prose with a memoir by Arthur Symons, New York, 1928.
Complete Poems, New York, 1928.
The Poetical works of Ernest Dowson, ed. Desmond Flower, Cassell, 1934, 1950 and 1967.
The Stories of Ernest Dowson, ed. Mark Longaker, Pennsylvania U. P., Philadelphia, 1947.
The Poems of Ernest Dowson, ed. Mark Longaker, Pennsylvania U. P., Philadelphia, 1962.
Ernest Dowson: Verses 1896 with Decorations 1899, ed R. K. R. Thornton and Ian Small, Woodstock, Oxford and New York, 1994.
Ernest Dowson: Collected Shorter Fiction, ed. Monica Borg and R. K. R. Thornton, Birmingham U. P., 2003.

Other reading

Victor Plarr, *Ernest Dowson 1888-1897: Reminiscences, Unpublished Letters and Marginalia*, Mathews, 1914.

W. R. Thomas, 'Ernest Dowson at Oxford', *Nineteenth Century*, CIII (April, 1928), 560-566.

Marion Plarr, *Cynara. The Story of Ernest and Adelaide*, 1933.

John Gawsworth, 'The Dowson Legend' in *Essays by Divers Hands*, n.s. vol XVII, ed. E. H. W. Meyerstein, 1938, reprinted as *The Dowson Legend*, 1939.

Mark Longaker, *Ernest Dowson*, Pennsylvania U. P., Philadelphia, 1944; revised 1945 and 1967.

Thomas Burnett Swann, *Ernest Dowson*, Twayne, New York, 1964.

The Letters of Ernest Dowson, ed. Desmond Flower and Henry Maas, Cassell, 1967.

John R. Reed, 'Bedlamite and Pierrot: Ernest Dowson's Esthetic of Futility', *ELH*, 35 (1968), 94-113.

Jonathan Ramsey, 'Ernest Dowson: an Annotated Bibliography of writings about him', *English Literature in Transition*, 14 (1971), 17-42.

Laurence Dakin, *Ernest Dowson, The Swan of Lee*, Warbrooke, Montreal 1972.

R. K. R. Thornton, *The Decadent Dilemma*, Arnold, 1983.

Chris Snodgrass, 'Ernest Dowson's Aesthetics of Contamination', *English Literature in Transition*, 26 (1983), 162-174.

New Letters from Ernest Dowson, ed. Desmond Flower, Whittington, Andoversford, 1984.

G. A. Cevasco, *Three Decadent Poets, Ernest Dowson, John Gray, and Lionel Johnson: An Annotated Bibliography*, Garland, New York, 1990.

Chris Snodgrass, 'Aesthetic Memory's Cul-de-sac: The Art of Ernest Dowson', *English Literature in Transition*, 35 (1992), 26-53.

R. K. R. Thornton, 'Ernest Dowson', *Dictionary of Literary Biography*, 135, Gale, Detroit, 1994, 96-105.

Jean-Jacques Chardin, *Ernest Dowson (1867-1900) et la crise fin de siècle anglaise*, Editions Messene, Paris, 1995.

Jad Adams, *Madder Music, Stronger Wine: The Life of Ernest Dowson, Poet and Decadent*, I. B. Tauris, 2000.

ALPHABETICAL LIST OF TITLES AND FIRST LINES